THE LITTLE BOOK OF

Restorative Justice

Revised and Updated

Published titles include:

The Little Book of Restorative Justice: Revised & Updated, by
Howard Zehr
The Little Book of Conflict Transformation,
by John Paul Lederach
The Little Book of Family Group Conferences,
New-Zealand Style, by Allan MacRae and Howard Zehr
The Little Book of Strategic Peacebuilding, by Lisa Schirch
The Little Book of Strategic Negotiation,
by Jayne Seminare Docherty
The Little Book of Circle Processes, by Kay Pranis
The Little Book of Contemplative Photography, by Howard Zehr
The Little Book of Restorative Discipline for Schools,
by Lorraine Stutzman Amstutz and Judy H. Mullet
The Little Book of Trauma Healing, by Carolyn Yoder
The Little Book of Biblical Justice, by Chris Marshall
The Little Book of Restorative Justice for People in Prison,
by Barb Toews
The Little Book of Cool Tools for Hot Topics,
by Ron Kraybill and Evelyn Wright
El Pequeño Libro De Justicia Restaurativa, by Howard Zehr
The Little Book of Dialogue, by Lisa Schirch and David Campt
The Little Book of Victim Offender Conferencing, by Lorraine S
Amstutz

Forthcoming titles or topics include:
Little Book of Restorative Justice for Sexual Abuse,
by Judah Oudshoorn with Michelle Jackett and Lorraine Stutzman
Amstutz
*The Big Book of Restorative Justice: Three Classic Justice & Peacebuilding
Books in One Volume,* by Howard Zehr, Lorraine S. Amstutz, Allan
Macrae, and Kay Pranis

The Little Books of Justice & Peacebuilding present, in highly
accessible form, key concepts and practices from the fields of restorative justice, conflict transformation, and peacebuilding. Written by
leaders in these fields, they are designed for practitioners, students,
and anyone interested in justice, peace, and conflict resolution.
The Little Books of Justice & Peacebuilding series is a coop-
erative effort between the Center for Justice and Peacebuilding of
Eastern Mennonite University (Howard Zehr, Series General Editor)
and publisher Good Books.

THE LITTLE BOOK OF
Restorative Justice

Revised and Updated

HOWARD ZEHR

Cover photograph by Howard Zehr

Design by Mike Bond

Good Books books may be purchased in bulk at special discounts for sales promotion, corporate gifts, fund-raising, or educational purposes. Special editions can also be created to specifications. For details, contact the Special Sales Department, Good Books, 307 West 36th Street, 11th Floor, New York, NY 10018 or info@skyhorsepublishing.com.

Good Books is an imprint of Skyhorse Publishing, Inc.®, a Delaware corporation.

Visit our website at www.goodbooks.com.

10 9 8 7 6 5 4 3 2 1

Library of Congress Cataloging-in-Publication Data

Zehr, Howard.
The little book of restorative justice : a bestselling book by one of the founders of the movement / Howard Zehr. -- Revised and updated.
pages cm
Includes bibliographical references.
ISBN 978-1-56148-823-0 (pbk.)
1. Restorative justice. 2. Victims of crimes. 3. Criminals--Rehabilitation. 4. Corrections--Philosophy. 5. Criminal justice, Administration of. I. Title. II. Title: Restorative justice.
HV8688.Z44 2014
364.6′8--dc23
2013042830

Printed in the United States of America

Table of Contents

Acknowledgments

A special thanks to the many friends and colleagues who gave me feedback on this manuscript. This includes my students, former students, and colleagues at the Center for Justice and Peacebuilding where I have taught since 1996. I especially want to thank Barb Toews, Jarem Sawatsky, Bonnie Price Lofton, Robert Gillette, Vernon Jantzi, Larissa Fast, and Ali Gohar for their careful attention and suggestions.

For this new edition, I am especially thankful to Sujatha Baliga for her careful reading and suggestions.

CHAPTER 1

An Overview

How should we as a society respond to wrongdoing? When a crime occurs, when an injustice or harm is committed, what needs to happen? What does justice require? The urgency of this question is emphasized daily by events reported in the media.

Whether we are concerned with crime or other offenses and harms, the Western legal system has profoundly shaped our thinking about these issues—not only in the Western world, but in much of the rest of the world as well.

The Western legal system's approach to justice has some important strengths. Yet there is also a growing acknowledgment of this system's limits and failures. Those who have been harmed, those who have caused harm, and community members in general often feel that the criminal justice process shaped by this legal system does not adequately meet their needs. Justice professionals—law enforcement officers, judges, lawyers, prosecutors, probation and parole officers, prison staff—frequently express a sense of frustration as well. Many feel that the criminal justice process deepens societal wounds and conflicts rather than contributing to healing or peace.

Restorative justice is an attempt to address some of these needs and limitations. Since the 1970s, a variety of programs and practices have emerged in thousands of communities and many countries throughout the world. Often these are offered as choices within or alongside the existing legal system, although in some occasions they are used as an alternative to the existing system. Since 1989, New Zealand has made restorative conferences the hub of its entire youth justice system.

In many places today, restorative justice is considered a sign of hope and the direction of the future. Whether it will live up to this promise remains to be seen, but many are optimistic.

Restorative justice began as an effort to deal with burglary and other property crimes that are usually viewed (often incorrectly) as relatively minor offenses. Today, however, restorative approaches are available in some communities for the most severe forms of criminal violence: death from drunken driving, assault, rape, even murder. Building upon the experience of the Truth and Reconciliation Commission in South Africa, efforts are also being made to apply a restorative justice framework to situations of mass violence.

These approaches and practices are also spreading beyond the criminal justice system to schools and universities, to the workplace, and to religious institutions. Some advocate the use of restorative approaches such as circles processes (a practice that emerged from First Nation communities in Canada) as a way to work through, resolve, and transform conflicts in general. Others pursue circle processes and other restorative approaches as a way to build and heal communities. Kay Pranis, a prominent restorative justice advocate, calls circles a form of participatory democracy that moves beyond simple majority rule.

In societies where Western legal systems have replaced and/or suppressed traditional justice and conflict-resolution processes, restorative justice is providing a framework to reexamine and sometimes reactivate these traditions. I sometimes envision restorative justice as a blend of key elements in modern human rights sensibilities and traditional approaches to harm or conflict.

Although the term "restorative justice" encompasses a variety of programs and practices, at its core it is a set of principles and values, a philosophy, an alternate set of guiding questions. Ultimately, restorative justice provides an alternative framework for thinking about wrongdoing. I will explore that framework in the pages that follow and illustrate how it translates into practice.

Why this *Little Book*?

In this *Little Book*, my intention is not to make the case for restorative justice. Nor do I explore the many implications of this approach. Rather, I intend this book to be a brief description or overview—the *CliffsNotes*, if you will—of restorative justice. Although I will outline some of the programs and practices of restorative justice, my focus in this book is especially the principles or philosophy of restorative justice. Other books in this *Little Books of Justice & Peacebuilding* series explore practice models more thoroughly; a list of these is provided at the end of this book.

The Little Book of Restorative Justice is for those who have heard the term and are curious about what it implies. But it is also an attempt to bring clarity to those of us involved in the field because it is so easy to lose clarity about our direction and what we have set out to do.

All social innovations have a tendency to lose their way as they develop and spread, and restorative justice is no different. With more and more programs being termed "restorative justice," the meaning of that phrase is sometimes diluted or confused.

> **Restorative justice claims to be victim-oriented.**

Under the inevitable pressures of working in the real world, restorative justice has sometimes been subtly coopted or diverted from its principles.

The victim advocacy community has been especially concerned about this. Restorative justice claims to be victim-oriented, but is it really? All too often, victim groups fear, restorative justice efforts have been motivated mainly by a desire to work with those who have offended in a more positive way. Like the criminal system that it aims to improve or replace, restorative justice may become primarily a way to deal with those who have offended.

Others wonder whether the field has adequately addressed the needs of those who have offended and made sufficient efforts to help them become their best selves. Do restorative justice programs give adequate support to those who have caused harm to carry out their obligations and to change their patterns of behavior? Do restorative justice programs adequately address the harms that may have led those who cause harm to become who they are? Are such programs becoming just another way to punish those who have harmed under a new guise? And what about the community at large? Is the community being adequately both allowed and encouraged to be involved and to assume its obligations?

Another concern is whether in articulating and practicing restorative justice, we are replicating patterns of racial and economic disparities that are prevalent in society. Is restorative justice as practiced in the United States, for example, being applied primarily for white folks? Is it adequately addressing underlying disparities?

Our past experience with change efforts in the justice arena warns us that sidetracks and diversions from our visions and models inevitably happen in spite of our best intentions. If advocates for change are unwilling to acknowledge and address these likely diversions, their efforts may end up much different than they intended. In fact, "improvements" can turn out to be worse than the conditions that they were designed to reform or replace.

One of the most important safeguards we can exert against such sidetracks is to give attention to core principles and values. If we are clear about principles and values, if we design our programs with these in mind, if we are open to being evaluated by these principles and values, we are much more likely to stay on track.

Put another way, the field of restorative justice has grown so rapidly and in so many directions that it is sometimes difficult to know how to move into the future with integrity and creativity. Only a clear vision of principles and goals can provide the compass we need as we find our way along a path that is inevitably winding and unclear.

This book is an effort to articulate the restorative justice concept and its principles in straightforward terms. However, I must acknowledge certain limits to the framework I will lay out here. Even though I have tried hard to remain critical and open, I come with a bias in favor of this ideal. Moreover, in spite of all efforts to the contrary, I write from my own "lens," and that is shaped by who I am: a white, middle-class male of European ancestry, a Christian, a Mennonite. This biography and these, as well as other, interests and values necessarily shape my voice and vision.

Even though there is somewhat of a consensus within the field about the broad outline of the principles of restorative justice, not all that follows is uncontested. What you read here is my understanding of restorative justice. It must be tested against the voices of others.

Finally, I've written this book within a North American context. The terminology, the issues raised, and even the way the concept is formulated reflect to some extent the realities of my setting. The first edition has been widely translated into other languages, but the translations needed for other contexts go beyond language.

With this background and these qualifications, then, what is "restorative justice"? So many misconceptions have grown up around the term that I find it increasingly important to first clarify what, in my view, restorative justice is *not*. Before I do that, however, I'll make a few comments about this revised edition.

About this revised edition

Much has happened since this book was first released in 2002. The book itself has sold more than 110,000 copies and has been translated and released in countries as disparate as Japan, the former Czechoslovakia, Pakistan, and Iran. As this suggests, the restorative justice field has continued to spread and develop over these years, and well beyond the criminal justice context. In fact, cities in the United Kingdom, New Zealand, South Korea, and elsewhere have been exploring what it means to become restorative cities. A few health care systems in the U.S. have adopted restoratively-oriented approaches to address cases of possible medical malpractice, allowing patients and doctors to interact much more freely in meeting needs and addressing obligations. Some advocates have argued that restorative justice is, in fact, a way of life.

Within the United States, at least, perhaps the biggest growth area for restorative justice has been in schools and, more recently, in the area of university conduct. This book tends to have a criminal justice focus, but several books in this *Little Books* series now address these educational contexts specifically.

Expansion has occurred within the criminal justice arena. The majority of U.S. states now have some reference to restorative justice principles or practices within their statutes and policies. Several countries have developed nation-wide models inspired by restorative justice. At the time of the first edition, most applications for using restorative justice for criminal cases came after there were formal charges. However, applications to keep cases out of the formal system, sometimes in an effort to address racial disparities, are now becoming more frequent.

Michelle Alexander's important book, *The New Jim Crow: Mass Incarceration in the Age of Colorblindness*, is bringing a much-needed awareness to the prevalence and implications of racial disparities within the American criminal justice system. This has appropriately heightened concerns about ways that restorative justice may be contributing to or replicating these patterns. Has the field adequately monitored this possibility? Have we given enough thought to how restorative justice might be proactively used to address this problem? Have we adequately considered the possibility of built-in biases and assumptions in the way we articulate and practice restorative justice? Have we encouraged and listened to diverse voices about what restorative justice should involve? These are urgent questions that this book cannot answer; hopefully, though, it can be a catalyst for discussion.

Increasingly, the labels "victim" and "offender" are being questioned. While these terms provide handy shorthand references and are common within the criminal justice system, they also tend to oversimplify and stereotype. In criminology, labeling theory has emphasized that labels are often judgmental and people may tend to become what they are labeled. Also, in many situations such as in schools, responsibility for wrongdoing may be unclear, or some responsibility may be shared by all participants; "victim" and "offender" labels may be especially inappropriate in these contexts. The alternates to these simple labels are often awkward, but in this edition, I have tried to minimize the use of these terms though I have not eliminated them.

One area of controversy has been the terminology of the overall field: should it be restorative *justice* or restorative *practices*? Restorative approaches are being used in many situations such as in schools or for problem-solving where the terminology of "justice" may not seem appropriate. I am pleased to see these applications and readily acknowledge the limits of the "justice" language. However, in my experience, most conflicts and harms involve an experience or perception of injustice, and I prefer not to lose awareness of the justice dimension. Thus I continue to use the term restorative "justice" in this book while acknowledging that restorative "practices" may be appropriate in some contexts.

Now, on to what, in my view, restorative justice is *not*.

Restorative justice *is not...*

- *Restorative justice is not primarily about forgiveness or reconciliation.*

    Some victims and victim advocates react negatively to restorative justice because they imagine that the goal of such programs is to encourage, or even to coerce, them to forgive or reconcile with those who have caused them and/or their loved ones harm.

    As we shall see, forgiveness or reconciliation is not a primary principle or focus of restorative justice. It is true that restorative justice does provide a context where either or both might happen. Indeed, some degree of forgiveness or even reconciliation—or at least a lessening of hostilities and fears—does seem to occur more frequently than in the adversarial setting of the criminal justice system. However, this is an experience that varies from participant to participant; it is entirely up to the individual. There should be no pressure to forgive or to seek reconciliation. Neither forgiveness nor reconciliation is a prerequisite to or a necessary outcome of restorative processes.

- **Restorative justice does not necessarily imply a return to past circumstances.**

    The term "restorative" is sometimes controversial because it can seem to imply a return to the past, as if the wrong or injury had not occurred. This is not likely to be possible, especially in the case of severe harm. Lynn Shiner, whose children were murdered, says "re-" words don't work: "I can't reorder anything because if I did, I would just pick up the scrambled pieces and put them back in order.... You build, you create a new life. I have a couple of pieces from my old life that I have to fit in."[1]

    In reality, a return to the past is rarely possible or even desirable. A person with a history of abuse or trauma or a long pattern of wrongdoing, for example, may not have a healthy personal or relational state to which to return. Their situation needs to be transformed, not restored. Similarly, restorative justice aims to transform, not perpetuate, patterns of racism and oppression.

    Restorative justice often involves movement toward a new sense of identity and health or new, healthier relationships. Many advocates see it as a way to restore a sense of hope and community to our world. In a recent email to me, restorative justice practitioner and attorney Fania Davis put it like this:

    > "It's not about returning to the pre-conflict status quo but about returning to one's best self that's always been there. When well facilitated, RJ processes create the possibility for transformation

of people, relationships, and communities. This is often a radical departure from the pre-conflict status quo. So what are we restoring? For me it's about returning to the part of us that really wants to be connected to one another in a good way. Returning to the goodness inherent in all of us. One might say returning to the divinity present in all of us. Or as indigenous elders put it, returning to that part of us which is related to all things."

- *Restorative justice is not mediation.*

  Like mediation programs, many restorative justice programs are designed around the possibility of a facilitated meeting or encounter between those harmed and those who caused harm, as well as perhaps some family and community members. However, an encounter is not always chosen or appropriate. Moreover, restorative approaches are important even when an offending party has not been identified or apprehended or when a party is unwilling or unable to meet. So restorative approaches are not limited to an encounter.

  Even when an encounter occurs, the term "mediation" is not a fitting description of that encounter. In a mediated conflict or dispute, parties are assumed to be on a level moral playing field, often with responsibilities that may need to be shared on all sides. While this sense of shared blame may be true in some criminal cases, in many cases it is not. Victims of rape or even burglaries do not want to be known as "disputants." In fact, they may well be struggling to overcome a tendency to blame themselves.

  At any rate, to participate in most restorative justice encounters, a wrongdoer must admit to some level of responsibility for the offense, and an important component of such programs is to name and acknowledge the wrongdoing. The "neutral" language of mediation may be misleading and even offensive in many cases.

Although the term "mediation" was adopted early on in the restorative justice field, it is increasingly being replaced by terms such as "conferencing" or "dialogue" for the reasons outlined above.

- ***Restorative justice is not primarily designed to reduce recidivism or repeat offenses.***

  In an effort to gain acceptance, restorative justice programs are often promoted or evaluated as ways to decrease repeat crimes.

  There are good reasons to believe that, in fact, such programs will reduce offending. Indeed, the research thus far is quite encouraging on this issue. Nevertheless, reduced recidivism is not the primary reason for operating restorative justice programs.

  Reduced recidivism is a byproduct, but restorative justice is done first of all because it is the right thing to do. Those who have suffered harm *should* be able to identify their needs and have them addressed; those who cause harm *should* be encouraged to take responsibility; and those affected by an offense *should* be involved in the process, regardless of whether the offending party gets the message and reduces their offending.

- ***Restorative justice is not a particular program or a blueprint.***

  Various programs embody restorative justice in part or in full. However, there is no pure model that can be seen as ideal or that can be simply implemented in

16

any community. Even after more than three decades of experience, we are still on a steep learning curve in this field. The most exciting practices that have emerged were not even imagined by those of us who began the first programs, and many more new ideas will surely emerge through dialogue and experimentation.

Also, all models are to some extent culture-bound. Consequently, restorative justice should be built from the bottom up, by communities, through dialogue, assessing their needs and resources, and applying the principles to their own situations.

> **Restorative justice is a compass, not a map.**

Restorative justice is *not a map,* but the principles of restorative justice can be seen as a *compass* offering direction. At a minimum, restorative justice is an invitation for dialogue and exploration.

- ***Restorative justice is not limited to "minor" offenses or first-time offenders.***

    It may be easier to get community support for programs that address so-called "minor" cases. However, experience has shown that restorative approaches may have the greatest impact in more severe cases. Moreover, if the principles of restorative justice are taken seriously, the need for restorative approaches is especially clear in severe cases. The guiding questions of restorative justice (see page 49) may help to tailor justice responses in very difficult situations. Domestic violence is one of the most challenging areas of application, and great caution is advised. Yet successful restorative approaches are emerging in this area as well.

Restorative approaches are challenging in all offenses where there are significant power imbalances, including hate crimes, bullying, and child sexual abuse. Program design must take this into account, and facilitators need to be thoroughly cross-trained in the underlying issues that give rise to the violence. But it can be done, and many argue that, when done well, it can produce better results than the way the current system is trying to resolve these issues.

It may seem that restorative justice programs are most appropriate for young people. However, restorative justice is equally applicable to adults, and many programs are designed for both.

• ***Restorative justice is not a new or North American development.***

The modern field of restorative justice developed in the 1970s from pilot projects in several North American communities. Seeking to apply their faith as well as their peace perspective to the harsh world of criminal justice, Mennonites and other practitioners (in Ontario, and later in Indiana) experimented with victim-offender encounters that led to programs in these communities and later became models for programs throughout the world. Restorative justice theory developed initially from these particular efforts.

However, the restorative justice movement did not develop out of a vacuum. It owes a great deal to earlier movements and to a variety of cultural and religious traditions. Many indigenous traditions had, and have, important restorative elements. The field owes a special debt to the Native people of North America and New Zealand for their contributions to the early development of the field, and other traditions are increasingly offering inspiration as well. The precedents and roots of restorative justice are much wider and deeper than the initiatives of the 1970s; they reach far back into human history.

- *Restorative justice is neither a panacea nor necessarily a replacement for the legal system.*

Restorative justice, as it is currently practiced, is by no means an answer to all situations. Nor is it clear that it should replace the legal system, even in an ideal world. Many feel that even if restorative justice could be widely implemented, some form of the Western legal system (ideally, a restoratively-oriented one) would still be needed as a backup and guardian of basic human

> **Restorative justice highlights personal and interpersonal dimensions of crime.**

rights. Indeed, this is the function that the youth courts play in the restorative juvenile justice system of New Zealand.

Most restorative justice advocates agree that crime has both a public dimension and a private dimension. Perhaps it would be more accurate to say that crime has a societal dimension, as well as a more personal and interpersonal dimension. The legal system focuses on the public dimension; that is, on society's interests and obligations as represented by the state. However, this emphasis downplays or ignores the personal and interpersonal aspects of crime. By putting a spotlight on and elevating the personal, interpersonal, and community dimensions of crime, restorative justice seeks to provide a better balance in how we experience justice.

- ***Restorative justice is not necessarily an alternative to prison.***

    Western society, and especially the United States, greatly overuses prisons. If restorative justice were taken seriously, our reliance on prisons would be reduced, and the nature of prisons would change significantly. However, restorative justice approaches may sometimes be used in conjunction with, or parallel to, prison sentences. Restorative justice can be an alternative to prison and, as such, could reduce our over-reliance on prison. It does not necessarily eliminate the need for some form of incarceration in some cases, however.

- ***Restorative justice is not necessarily the opposite of retribution.***

    Despite my earlier writing, I no longer see restoration as the polar opposite of retribution, though it should reduce our reliance on punishment for its own sake. More on that later on page 75.

Restorative justice *is* concerned about needs and roles

The restorative justice movement originally began as an effort to rethink the needs that crimes create as well as the roles implicit in crimes. Restorative justice advocates were concerned about needs that were not being met in the usual justice process. They also believed that the prevailing understanding of who the legitimate participants or stakeholders are in justice was too restrictive.

Restorative justice expands the circle of stakeholders—those with a stake or standing in the event or the case—beyond just the government and the offending party to include those who have been directly victimized as well as community members.

Because this view of needs and roles was at the origin of the movement, and because the needs/roles framework is so basic to the concept, it is important to start this review there. As the field has developed, stakeholder analysis has become more complex and encompassing.

> **Restorative justice expands the circle of stakeholders.**

The following discussion is limited to some of the core concerns that were present at the beginning of the movement and that continue to play a central role. It is also limited to "justice needs"—the needs of those harmed, of those causing harm, and of community members—that might be met, at least partially, through a justice process.

Victims: those who have been harmed

Of special concern to restorative justice in a criminal justice context are the needs of crime victims that are not being adequately met by the criminal justice system. People who have been victimized often feel ignored, neglected, or even abused by the justice process. Sometimes, in fact, the state's interests are in direct conflict with those of victims. This results in part from the legal definition of crime, which does not directly include victims themselves. Crime is defined as against the state, so the state takes the place of the victims. Yet those who have been harmed often have a number of specific needs from the justice process.

Due to the legal definition of crime and the nature of the criminal justice process, the following four types of needs seem to be especially neglected:

1. **Information**. Those who have experienced harm need answers to questions they have about the offense or the offender, including why and how the offense happened and what has happened since. They need *real* information, not speculation or the legally constrained information that comes from a trial or plea agreement. Securing real information usually requires direct or indirect access to the one who caused the harm and holds this information.

2. **Truth-telling**. An important element in healing or transcending the experience of crime is an opportunity to tell the story of what happened. There are good therapeutic reasons for this. Part of the trauma of crime is the way it upsets our views of ourselves and our world—our life-stories. Transcendence of these experiences means "restorying" our lives by telling the stories in significant settings, often where they can receive public acknowledgment. Often, too, it is important for those victimized to tell their stories to the ones who caused the harm and to have them understand the impact of their actions.

3. **Empowerment**. People who have been victimized often feel like control has been taken away from them by the offenses they've

experienced—control over their properties, their bodies, their emotions, their dreams. Involvement in their own cases as they go through the justice process can be an important way to return a sense of empowerment to them. The opportunity and encouragement to self-identify their own needs is also important—rather than have them defined by the state or even victim advocates.

4. **Restitution or vindication**. Restitution by those who have caused harm is often important to those harmed, sometimes because of the actual losses, but just as importantly, because of the symbolic recognition restitution implies. When someone who has caused harm makes an effort to make right the harm, even if only partially, it is a way of saying, "I am taking responsibility, and you are not to blame."

    Restitution, in fact, is a symptom or sign of a more basic need, the need for vindication. While the concept of vindication is beyond the scope of this booklet, I am convinced that it is a basic need that we all have when we are treated unjustly.

    > **Victims should be able to identify their own needs.**

    Restitution is one of a number of ways of meeting this need to even the score. Apology may also help meet this need to have one's harm recognized.

The theory and practice of restorative justice have emerged from and been profoundly shaped by an effort to take these "justice needs" of victims seriously.[2]

Offenders: those who have caused harm

A second major area of concern that gave rise to restorative justice is ensuring accountability for those who have caused harm.

The criminal justice system is concerned about holding offenders accountable, but accountability in that system means making sure those who cause harm get the punishment they deserve. Little in the process encourages them to understand the consequences of their actions or to empathize with those they have harmed. On the contrary, the adversarial game requires them to look out for themselves. Those who have offended are discouraged from acknowledging their responsibility and are given little opportunity to act on this responsibility in concrete ways. Indeed, the risk of lengthy prison sentences acts as a disincentive to truth telling.

The neutralizing strategies—the stereotypes and rationalizations that those who offend often use to distance themselves from the people they hurt—are never challenged. Unfortunately, then, their sense of alienation from society is only heightened by the legal process and by the prison experience; indeed, they often feel like victims of the system and society. For a variety of reasons, then, the legal process tends to discourage responsibility and empathy on the part of those who have offended.

Restorative justice has brought an awareness of the limits and negative byproducts of punishment. Beyond that, however, it has argued that punishment is not real accountability. Real accountability involves facing up to what one has done. It means encouraging those who have caused harm to understand the impact of their behavior—the harms they have done—and urging them to take steps to put things as right as possible. This

24

accountability, it is argued, is better for those who have been victimized, better for those who have caused harm, and better for society as well.

Those who have caused harm have other needs beyond their responsibilities to victims and communities. If we expect them to assume their responsibilities, to change their behavior, and to become contributing members of our communities, their needs, says restorative justice, must be addressed as well. That subject is beyond the scope of this *Little Book*, but the following suggests some of what is needed.

Those who have caused harm need justice to provide:

1. Accountability
   - that addresses the resulting harms,
   - encourages empathy and responsibility,
   - and transforms shame.[3]

2. Encouragement to experience personal transformation including
   - healing for the harms that contributed to their offending behavior, including personal and historical traumas;[4]
   - opportunities for treatment for addictions and/or other problems;
   - and enhancement of personal competencies.

3. Encouragement and support for integration into the community.

4. For a small number, at least temporary restraint.

Community

Communities and their members have needs arising from crime, and they have roles to play. Restorative justice advocates, such as former judge Barry Stuart and Kay Pranis, argue that when the state takes over in our name, it undermines our sense of community.[5] Communities are impacted by crime and, in many cases, should be considered stakeholders as secondary victims. Communities may also have responsibilities to victims, to offenders, and to others who are part of the community.

When a community becomes involved in a case, it can initiate a forum to work at these matters, while strengthening the community itself. This topic, too, is a large one. The following list suggests some areas of concern.

Communities need justice to provide:

1. Attention to their concerns as victims.

2. Opportunities to build a sense of community and mutual accountability.

3. Opportunities and encouragement to take on their obligations for the welfare of their members, including those who have been harmed and those who caused harm, and to foster the conditions that promote healthy communities.

Much more has been written about who has a stake in a crime and about their needs and roles. However, the basic concerns about the needs and roles of victims, offenders, and community members outlined above continue to provide the focus for both the theory and practice of restorative justice.

Restorative justice focuses on needs more than deserts.

In short, the legal or criminal justice system centers on offenders and deserts—making sure those who offend get what they *deserve*. Restorative justice is more focused on *needs*: the needs of those harmed, of those causing harm, and of the communities in which these situations arise.

CHAPTER 2

Restorative Principles

Restorative justice is based upon an old, common-sense understanding of wrongdoing. Although it would be expressed differently in different cultures, this approach is probably common to most traditional societies. For those of us from a European background, it is the way many of our ancestors (and perhaps even our parents) understood wrongdoing.

- *"Crime" or wrongdoing is a violation of people and of interpersonal relationships.*

- *Violations create obligations.*

- *The central obligation is to put right the wrongs, i.e., to repair the harms caused by wrongdoing.*

Underlying this understanding of wrongdoing is an assumption about society: we are all interconnected. In the Hebrew scriptures, this is embedded in the concept of *shalom*, the vision of living in a sense of "all-rightness" with each other, with the creator, and with the environment. Many cultures have a word that represents this notion of the centrality of relationships. For the Maori, it is communicated by *whakapapa*; for the Navajo, *hozho*; for many Africans, the Bantu word *ubuntu*; for Tibetan Buddhists, *tendrel*. Although the specific meanings of these words vary, they communicate a similar message: all things are connected to each other in a web of relationships.

In this worldview, the problem of crime—and wrongdoing in general—is that it represents a wound in the community, a tear in the web of relationships. Crime represents damaged relationships. In fact, damaged relationships are both a *cause* and an *effect* of crime. Many traditions have a saying that a harm to one

> ## A harm to one is a harm to all.

is a harm to all. A harm such as crime ripples out to disrupt the whole web. Moreover, wrongdoing is often a symptom of something that is out of balance in the web.

Interrelationships imply mutual obligations and responsibilities. It comes as no surprise, then, that this view of wrongdoing emphasizes the importance of making amends or of "putting right." Indeed, making amends for wrongdoing is an obligation. While the initial emphasis may be on the obligations owed by those who have caused harm, the focus on interconnectedness opens the possibility that others—especially the larger community—may have obligations as well.

Even more fundamentally, this view of wrongdoing implies a concern for healing of those involved—those directly harmed, those who cause harm, and their communities.

How does this understanding compare or contrast with the "legal" or criminal justice understanding of crime? The differences in these two approaches might be boiled down to three central questions asked in the search for justice as shown in the accompanying chart.

Two different views

Criminal justice	Restorative justice
• Crime is a violation of the law and the state.	• Crime is a violation of people and relationships.
• Violations create guilt.	• Violations create obligations.
• Justice requires the state to determine blame (guilt) and impose pain (punishment).	• Justice involves victims, offenders, and community members in an effort to repair the harm, to "put things right."
• *Central focus: offenders getting what they deserve.*	• *Central focus: victim needs and offender responsibility for repairing harm.*

Three different questions

Criminal justice	Restorative justice
• What laws have been broken?	• Who has been harmed?
	• What are their needs?
• Who did it?	• Whose obligations are these?
• What do they deserve?	

In an oft-quoted passage from Christian and Jewish scripture, the prophet Micah asks the question, "What does the Lord require?" The answer begins with the phrase, "To do justice." But what does justice require? As we have seen, Western society's answer has focused on making sure those who have offended get what they deserve. *Restorative justice answers differently, focusing first of all on needs and associated obligations.*

Appendix I provides a fuller statement of restorative justice principles and their implications, based directly on the concept of wrongdoing outlined above. For our purposes here, however, the concept of interrelatedness is basic to understanding why needs, roles, and obligations are so essential to restorative justice.

Three pillars of restorative justice

Three central concepts or pillars deserve a closer look: *harms and needs*, *obligations*, and *engagement*.

1. Restorative justice focuses on *harm*.

Restorative justice understands crime first of all as harm done to people and communities. Our legal system, with its focus on rules and laws

31

and with its view that the state is the victim, often loses sight of this reality.

Concerned primarily with making sure those who offend get what they deserve, the legal system usually considers those victimized as, at best, a secondary concern of justice. Focusing on harm, on the contrary, implies an inherent concern for the needs and roles of those who have been harmed.

For restorative justice, then, justice begins with a concern for victims and their needs. It seeks to repair the harm as much as possible, both concretely and symbolically. This victim-oriented approach requires that justice be concerned about victims' needs even when no offender has been identified or apprehended. And it is important that those who have been harmed are provided an opportunity to define

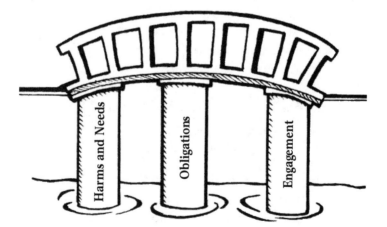

their needs rather than having others or a system define needs for them.

While our first concern must be the harm experienced by victims, the focus on harm implies that we also need to be concerned about harms experienced by those who have caused the harm as well as communities. This may require us to address the root causes of crime. The goal of restorative justice is to provide an experience of healing for all concerned. And ideally, restorative justice is about prevention of harm as well as justice after harm has occurred.

2. Wrongs or harms result in *obligations*.

For this reason, restorative justice emphasizes accountability and responsibility for those who cause harm.

The legal system defines accountability as making sure those who offend are punished. If crime is essentially about harm, however, accountability means they should be encouraged to understand that harm. Those who have caused harm should begin to comprehend the consequences of their behavior. Moreover, it means they have a responsibility to repair the harm, making things right as much as possible, both concretely and symbolically. That is, they have a responsibility to do right by the people they harmed. This is not only the "right" thing to do but is more likely than punishment to deter future offending.

As we shall see, the first obligation is on those who are directly responsible for the harm, but the community and society have obligations as well.

3. Restorative justice promotes *engagement or participation.*

The principle of engagement suggests that the primary parties affected by crime—those who have been victimized, those who have offended, and members of the community—are provided significant roles in the justice process. These "stakeholders" need to be given information about each other and need to be involved in deciding what justice requires in this case.

In some cases, this may mean actual dialogue between these parties, as happens in victim offender conferences. They share their stories and come to a consensus about what should be done. In other cases, it may involve indirect exchanges, the use of surrogates, or other forms of involvement.

The principle of engagement implies involvement of an enlarged circle of parties as compared to the traditional justice process.

So restorative justice is constructed upon three simple elements or pillars: *harms and related needs* (of those victimized, first of all, but also of the communities and those who cause harm); *obligations* that have resulted from (and given rise to) this harm (offender's, but also the community's); and *engagement* of those who have a legitimate interest or stake in the offense and its resolution (those harmed, those causing harm, and community members). Ross London has argued that "the soul of RJ is the effort to repair the harm of crime."[1]

Below, in summary, is a skeletal outline of restorative justice. Although it is inadequate by itself, it provides a framework upon which a fuller understanding can be built.

> Restorative justice requires, at minimum, that we address the harms and needs of those harmed, hold those causing harm accountable to "put right" those harms, and involve both of these parties as well as relevant communities in this process.

The "how" and the "who" are important

Who is involved in the justice process, and how they are involved, is an important part of restorative justice.

Process—the "how"

Our legal system is an adversarial process conducted by professionals who stand in for the offender and the state, refereed by a judge. Outcomes are imposed by authorities—laws, judges, or juries—who stand outside the essential conflict. Victims, community members, and even offenders rarely participate in this process in any substantial way.

Although restorative justice usually recognizes the need for outside authorities and, in some cases, imposed outcomes, it prefers *processes that are collaborative and inclusive* and *outcomes that are mutually agreed upon rather than imposed.*

Restorative justice often acknowledges a place for the adversarial approach and the role of professionals as well as an important role for the state. However, restorative justice emphasizes the importance of participation by those who have a direct stake in the event or offense— that is, those who are involved, impacted by, or who otherwise have a legitimate interest in the offense.

> **Restorative justice prefers inclusive, collaborative processes and consensual outcomes.**

A direct, facilitated, face-to-face encounter—with adequate screening, preparation, and safeguards—is often an ideal forum for the participation of the particular stakeholders. As we shall see shortly, this can take a variety of forms: a victim offender conference, a family group conference, or a circle process.

A meeting allows those harmed and those causing harm to give faces to each other, to ask questions of each other directly, to negotiate together how to put things right. It provides an opportunity for those who have been victimized to ask questions or to directly tell the one who victimized them the impact of the offense. It allows those who have offended to hear and to begin to understand the effects of their behavior. It offers possibilities for acceptance of responsibility and apology. Many of those who been victimized, as well as those who have offended, have found such a meeting to be a powerful and positive experience.

An encounter—direct or indirect—is not always possible, and, in some cases, may not be desirable. In some cultures, a direct encounter may be inappropriate. An indirect encounter might include a letter, a video exchange, or meeting with a person who represents the victim. In all cases, efforts should be made to provide maximum involvement of the stakeholders and exchange of information between them.

Stakeholders—the "who"

The key stakeholders, of course, are those who have been directly harmed and those who caused the harm. Members of the community may be directly affected, too, and thus should also be considered immediate stakeholders. In addition to this circle, there are others who have varying degrees of stake in the situation. These may include family members and friends of the victim or other "secondary victims"; families or friends of those who caused the harm; or other members of the community.

Who is the community?

Controversy has arisen within the restorative justice field about the meaning of community and how actually to involve the community in these processes. The issue is particularly a problem in cultures where traditional communities have eroded, as is true in much of the United States. Furthermore, "community" can be too abstract a concept to be useful. And a community can be guilty of abuses. A discussion of these issues is beyond the scope of this book, but a few observations may be helpful.[2]

In practice, restorative justice has tended to focus on "communities of care" or micro-communities. There are communities of *place*, where people live near and interact with each other, but there are also networks of relationships that are not geographically defined. For restorative justice, the key questions are: 1) who in the community cares about these people or about this offense, and 2) how can we involve them in the process?

It may be helpful to differentiate between "community" and "society." Restorative justice has tended to focus on the micro-communities of place or relationships that are directly affected by an offense but are often neglected by "state justice." However, there are larger concerns and obligations that belong to society beyond those who have a direct stake in a particular event. These include a society's concern for the safety, human rights, and general well-being of its members. Many argue that the government has an important and legitimate role in looking after such societal concerns.[3]

Restorative justice aims to put things right

We have discussed so far the needs and roles of stakeholders. More needs to be said, however, about the *goals* of restorative justice.

Addressing harm

Central to restorative justice is the idea of making things right or, to use a more active phrase often used in British English, "putting right." It is the opportunity and encouragement for those who have caused harm to do right by those they have harmed. As already noted, this implies a responsibility on the part of the offending person or persons to, as much as possible, take active steps to repair the harm to those harmed (and perhaps the impacted community). In cases such as murder, the harm obviously cannot be repaired; however, symbolic steps, including acknowledgment of responsibility or restitution, can be helpful to surviving family members and loved ones—or "co-victims"—and are a responsibility of offenders.

Putting right implies reparation or restoration or recovery, but these "re-" words are often inadequate. When a severe wrong has been committed, there is no possibility of repairing the harm or going back to what was before.

It is possible that some-one who has been harmed may be helped toward heal-ing when the one causing the

> **Restorative justice seeks to "make things right."**

harm works toward making things right—whether con-cretely or symbolically. Many crime victims, however, are ambivalent about the term "healing," because of the sense of finality or termination that it connotes. This journey belongs to victims—no one else can walk it for them—but an effort to put right can assist in this process, although it can never fully restore.

The obligation to put right is first of all the responsi-bility of those who have caused the harm. However, the community may have responsibilities as well—to those harmed, but perhaps also to those causing harm. For those responsible for the harm to successfully carry out their obligations, they may need support and encour-agement from the wider community. Moreover, the community has responsibilities for the situations that are causing or encouraging crime. Ideally, restorative justice processes can provide a catalyst and/or a forum for exploring and assigning these needs, responsibilities, and expectations.

Addressing causes

Putting right requires that we address the harms but also the *causes* of crime. Many people who have been victimized want this. They want to know that steps are being taken to reduce such harms to themselves and others.

Family group conferences in New Zealand, where restorative justice is the norm for youth justice, are expected to develop a consensually-supported plan that includes elements for both reparation and prevention. These plans must speak to the needs of those victimized and to the obligations of the offending person or persons to address those needs. But the plan must also address what those who have offended need in order to change their behaviors.

Those who offend have an obligation to address the causes of their behavior, but they usually cannot do this alone. Moreover, there may be larger obligations beyond those that are the direct responsibility of the one who has caused the harm. Social injustices and other conditions that cause crime or create unsafe conditions are in part the responsibility of families, communities, and the larger society.

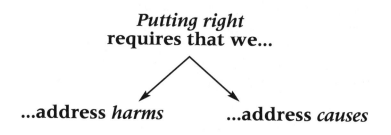

Putting right **requires that we...**

...address *harms*   **...address *causes***

Offenders as victims

If we are to truly address harms and causes, we must explore the harms that those who cause harm have themselves experienced.

Studies show that many of those who offend have indeed been victimized or traumatized in significant ways. And even when they have not been directly victimized, many people who offend perceive themselves to be victims. These harms and perceptions of harms may be an important contributing cause of crime. In fact, Harvard professor and former prison psychiatrist James Gilligan has argued that all violence is an effort to achieve justice or to undo injustice.[4] In other words, much crime may be a response to—or an effort to undo—a sense of victimization.

A perception of oneself as victim does not absolve responsibility for offending behavior. However, if Gilligan is right, we cannot expect offending behavior to stop without addressing this sense of victimization. In fact, punishment often reinforces the sense of victimization.

Sometimes offenders are satisfied when their sense of being victims is simply acknowledged. Sometimes their perception of being victims must be challenged. Sometimes the damage done must be repaired before they can be expected to change their behavior.

This is a controversial topic and especially difficult, understandably, for those who have been victims of crime but have done little or no harm to others in their lives. Too often these reasoned arguments sound like excuses. Moreover, why do some people who are victimized turn to crime and others do not? Nevertheless, I am convinced that any attempt to reduce the causes of offending will require us to explore offenders' experiences of victimization.

In this exploration, instead of using the loaded language of victimization, it may be more helpful to speak of "trauma." In her book *Creating Sanctuary*, psychiatrist

Restorative justice balances concern for all.

Sandra Bloom makes the point that unresolved trauma tends to be reenacted. If it is not adequately dealt with, trauma is reenacted in the lives of those who experience the trauma, in their families, even in future generations.[5]

Trauma is a core experience not only of those victimized, but also of many who offend. Much violence may actually be a reenactment of trauma that was experienced earlier but not responded to adequately. Society tends to respond by delivering more trauma in the form of imprisonment. While the realities of trauma must not be used to excuse, they must be understood, and they must be addressed.

In summary, an effort to put right the wrongs is the hub or core of restorative justice. Putting right has two dimensions: 1) addressing the harms that have been done, and 2) addressing the causes of those harms, including the contributing harms.

Since justice should seek to put right, and since victims have been harmed, *restorative justice must start with those who have been victimized* and their needs.

However, restorative justice is ultimately concerned about the restoration and reintegration of those who have been harmed, those who have caused harm, and the well-being of the entire community. Restorative justice is about balancing concern for all parties.

> **Restorative justice encourages outcomes that promote responsibility, reparation, and healing for all.**

A restorative lens

Restorative justice seeks to provide an alternate framework or lens for thinking about crime and justice.

Principles

This restorative lens or philosophy can be envisioned around five key principles or actions:

1. Focus on the harms and consequent needs of those harmed first of all, but also on those of the community and of those causing harm;

2. Address the obligations that result from those harms (the obligations of the offending persons, as well as those of the community and society);

3. Use inclusive, collaborative processes;

4. Involve those with a legitimate stake in the situation, including those victimized, those offending, community members, and society;

5. Seek to repair the harm and put right the wrongs to the extent possible.

We might diagram restorative justice as a wheel. At the hub is the central focus of restorative justice: seeking to put right the wrongs and harms. Each of the spokes represents the four other essential elements outlined above: focusing on harms and needs, addressing obligations, involving stakeholders (victims, offenders, and communities), and, to the extent possible, using collaborative, inclusive processes. This needs to be done, of course, in an attitude of respect for all involved.

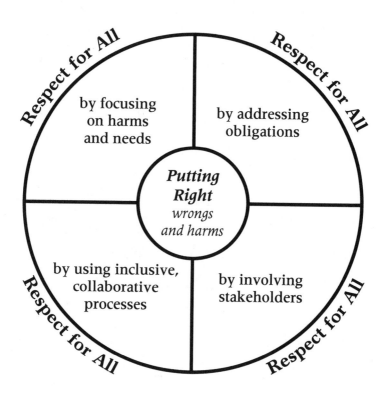

To use an image that is more organic, we might diagram restorative justice as a flower. In the center is the central focus: putting right. Each of the petals represents one of the principles required to succeed in putting right.

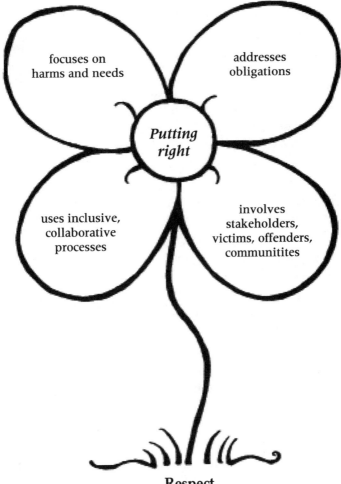

Values

The principles of restorative justice are useful only if they are rooted in a number of underlying values. Too often these values are unstated and taken for granted. However, to apply restorative justice principles in a way that is true to their spirit and intent, we must be explicit about these values. Otherwise, for example, we might use a restoratively-based process but arrive at non-restorative outcomes.

The principles of restorative justice—the hub and the spokes—must be surrounded by a rim of values in order to function properly. The principles that make up the restorative justice flower must be rooted in values in order to flourish.

As I noted earlier, underlying restorative justice is the vision of interconnectedness. Whether we realize it or not, we are all connected to each other and to the larger world through a web of relationships. When this web is disrupted, we are all affected. The primary elements of restorative justice—harm and need, obligation, and participation—derive from this vision.

But as Jarem Sawatsky has pointed out, this value of interconnectedness must be balanced by an appreciation for particularity.[6] Although we are connected, we are not the same. Particularity appreciates diversity. It respects the individuality and worth of each person. It takes seriously specific contexts and situations.

Justice must acknowledge both our interconnections and our individuality. The value of particularity reminds us that context, culture, and personality are all important.

Much more could be and has been written about the values underlying restorative justice. In fact, perhaps one of restorative justice's greatest attributes is the way it encourages us to explore our values together.

Ultimately, however, one basic value is supremely important: respect. If I had to put restorative justice into one word, I would choose respect: respect for all—even those who are different from us, even those who seem to be our enemies. Respect reminds us of our interconnectedness but also of our differences. Respect insists

> **Restorative justice is respect.**

that we balance concern for all parties. Respect can help us to recognize and address unjust hierarchies of power.

If we pursue justice as respect, treating all equally, we will do justice restoratively.

If we do not respect others, we will not do justice restoratively, no matter how earnestly we adopt the principles.

The value of respect underlies restorative justice principles and must guide and shape their application.

Defining restorative justice

How, then, should restorative justice be defined? Even though there is general agreement on the basic outlines of restorative justice, those in the field have been unable to come to a consensus on its specific meaning. Some of us question the wisdom or usefulness of such a definition. While we recognize the need for principles and benchmarks, we worry about the arrogance and finality of establishing a rigid meaning. With these concerns in mind, I offer the following as a working definition of restorative justice.[7]

> Restorative justice is an approach to achieving justice that involves, to the extent possible, those who have a stake in a specific offense or harm to collectively identify and address harms, needs, and obligations in order to heal and put things as right as possible.

The goals of restorative justice

In her excellent handbook, *Restorative Justice: A Vision for Healing and Change,* Susan Sharpe summarizes the goals and tasks of restorative justice in this way:[8]

Restorative justice programs aim to:

- *put key decisions into the hands of those most affected by crime;*

- *make justice more healing and, ideally, more transformative;*

- *reduce the likelihood of future offenses.*

Achieving these goals requires that:

- *victims are involved in the process and come out of it satisfied;*

- *offenders understand how their actions have affected other people and take responsibility for those actions;*

- *outcomes help to repair the harms done and address the reasons for the offenses (specific plans are tailored to the victims' and the offenders' needs);*

- *victims and offenders both gain a sense of "closure,"* [9] *and both are reintegrated into the community.*

Guiding questions of restorative justice

Ultimately, restorative justice boils down to a set of questions that we need to ask when a wrong occurs. These guiding questions are, in fact, the essence of restorative justice.

Guiding questions of restorative justice

1. Who has been harmed?

2. What are their needs?

3. Whose obligations are these?

4. Who has a stake in this situation?

5. What are the causes?

6. What is the appropriate process to involve stakeholders in an effort to put things right and address underlying causes?

If we think of restorative justice as a particular program, or a set of programs, we soon find it difficult to apply those programs to a broad variety of situations. For example, the forms of victim offender conferencing being used for "ordinary" crimes may have little direct application in cases of mass, societal violence. Without careful safeguards, restorative justice models of practice may be dangerous if applied to situations of patterned violence and imbalances of power like domestic violence.

If we instead employ the guiding questions that shape restorative justice, we find restorative justice to be applicable to a wide range of situations. The guiding questions of restorative justice can help us to reframe issues, to think beyond the confines that legal justice has created for society, and to "change our lenses" on wrongdoing.

These guiding questions are causing some defense attorneys in the U.S. to rethink their roles and obligations in death penalty cases. Defense victim outreach (DVO, formerly DIVO) has emerged as an effort to incorporate survivors' needs and concerns in trials and their outcomes by giving survivors access to the defense, as well as the prosecution. This approach also seeks to encourage defendants to take appropriate responsibility in these cases. A number of plea agreements have been reached that were based on victims' needs and that allowed offenders to accept responsibility.

Many victim advocates are deeply concerned about the dangers of victim-offender encounters in situations of domestic violence. These concerns are legitimate; there are profound dangers in an encounter where a pattern of violence continues or where cases are not being carefully monitored by people trained in domestic violence. Some would argue that encounters are never appropriate. Others, including some victims of domestic violence, argue that encounters are important and powerful in the right situations and with appropriate safeguards. In recent years, successful programs using a restorative approach have been developed in some communities.

But whether or not encounters are appropriate in situations like domestic violence, the guiding questions of restorative justice can help sort out what needs to be done without getting stuck on—and limited to—the question, "What does the offender deserve?" When faced with a new situation

> **Restorative justice involves changing our questions.**

or application, I often turn to these questions as a guide.

The guiding questions of restorative justice may, in fact, be viewed as restorative justice in a nutshell.

Signposts of restorative justice

As we begin to think of practical applications of restorative justice, another guide is provided by the following ten principles or signposts. These principles can be of use in designing or evaluating programs. Like the guiding questions, they may be useful in crafting responses to specific cases or situations.

Signposts of restorative justice[10]

1. Focus on the harms of wrongdoing rather than the rules that have been broken.

2. Show equal concern and commitment to those victimized and those who have offended, involving both in the process of justice.

3. Work toward the restoration of those harmed, empowering them and responding to their needs as they see them.

4. Support those who have offended, while encouraging them to understand, accept, and carry out their obligations.

5. Recognize that while obligations may be difficult for those who have offended, those obligations should not be intended as harms, and they must be achievable.

6. Provide opportunities for dialogue, direct or indirect, between those harmed and those who have harmed, as desired by both parties.

7. Find meaningful ways to involve the community and to respond to the community bases of crime.

8. Encourage collaboration and reintegration of both those who are harmed and those who harmed, rather than relying upon coercion and isolation.

9. Give attention to the unintended consequences of actions and programs.

10. Show respect to all parties—those harmed, those who harmed, their friends and loved ones, and justice colleagues.

CHAPTER 3

Restorative
Practices

T he concept and philosophy of restorative justice
emerged during the 1970s and '80s in the United
States and Canada in conjunction with a practice
that was then called the Victim Offender Reconciliation
Program (VORP). Since then, VORP has been modi-
fied and usually renamed, new forms of practice have
appeared, and older programs have been reshaped and
renamed "restorative." What are the main approaches or
practices currently being used within the Western criminal justice field? Be aware that the applications in the
criminal justice arena that I cite here are by no means
the whole picture.

Schools have become an important area of restorative practices. While there are some similarities to restorative justice programs for criminal cases, the approaches used in an educational setting must necessarily be shaped to fit that context. (Two *Little Books* in this series address these settings; see Additional Reading at the end of this book.)

Restorative approaches are also being adapted to the workplace and to larger community issues and processes. Again, there are similarities to the models outlined below, but there are also important differences. Restorative justice also has become part of the conversation about how to approach "transitional justice," e.g., following large-scale, societal conflicts and wrongdoing. The focus below, however, is on approaches in a criminal justice context.

For those who come from societies closer to traditional ways—in Africa, for example, or in North American indigenous communities—restorative justice often serves as a catalyst to reevaluate, resurrect, legitimate, and adapt older, customary approaches. During colonization, the Western legal model often condemned and repressed traditional forms of justice that, although not perfect, were highly functional for those societies.

Restorative justice can provide a conceptual framework to affirm and legitimate what was good about those traditions and to develop adapted models that can operate within the realities of the modern legal system. In fact, two of the most important forms of restorative justice—family group conferences and peacemaking circles—are adaptations (but not replications) of these traditional ways.

Restorative justice is also providing a concrete way to think about justice within the theory and practice of conflict transformation and peacebuilding. Most conflicts revolve around, or at least involve, a sense of injustice. Although the field of conflict resolution or conflict transformation has acknowledged

> **Restorative justice aids conflict transformation and peacebuilding.**

this somewhat, the concept and practice of justice in this area has been fairly vague. The principles and practices of restorative justice can provide a concrete framework for addressing justice issues within a conflict. (See Appendix V.)

For example, after taking a restorative justice course in our Summer Peacebuilding Institute, several African practitioners returned to Ghana where they had previously been trying to help resolve a protracted conflict. Drawing upon the restorative justice framework, they were able, for the first time, to address the justice issues in the conflict, using their traditional community justice process. As a result, the peacemaking effort came unstuck and began to move forward.

Similarly, several Pakistani practitioners who graduated from our program have returned to Pakistan and found the restorative justice model helpful for enlightening and updating their traditional *jirga* process for decision-making and conflict resolution.

The restorative justice field is becoming too diverse to capture it in any simple classification. Moreover, the various models described below are often blended, making clear distinctions between them difficult. The following, however, is an attempt to provide a brief overview of some of its emerging practices within the Western criminal justice arena. A separate *Little Book* is available for each of these models, describing them in much more detail. (See Additional Reading.)

Core approaches often involve a facilitated encounter

Three distinct models have tended to dominate the practice of restorative justice: victim offender conferences, family group conferences, and circle processes. Increasingly, however, these models are being blended. Family group conferences may utilize a circle, and new forms with elements of each are being developed for certain circumstances. In some cases, several models may be used in a single case or situation. A victim offender encounter may be held prior to and in preparation for a sentencing circle, for example.

All of these models have important elements in common, however. Each of these models involves a facilitated encounter or dialogue

Models are often blended.

between key stakeholders— those harmed and those causing harm, at minimum, and perhaps other community and justice people as well. Sometimes, if an encounter between a victim and an offender is impossible or inappropriate, representatives or surrogates may be used. Sometimes letters or videos are used in preparation for, or in place of, a direct meeting. All of these models, however, involve some form of encounter and dialogue, with a preference for face-to-face meetings.

These encounters are led by trained facilitators who guide the process, balancing concern for all the parties involved. Unlike arbitrators, conference or circle facilitators do not impose settlements. Each model allows an opportunity for participants to explore facts, feelings, and resolutions. They are encouraged to tell their stories, to ask questions, to express their feelings, and to work toward mutually acceptable outcomes.

Ron Claassen, a longtime restorative justice practitioner, has noted that to resolve any type of wrongdoing, three things have to happen:[1]

1. The wrong or injustice must be acknowledged;

2. Equity needs to be created or restored;

3. Future intentions need to be addressed.

An encounter provides an opportunity for the wrongdoing to be articulated by those harmed and acknowledged by those who caused the harm. Outcomes such as restitution or apology help to right the balance—that is, to establish or restore equity.

Questions about the future usually need to be discussed: Will the person who caused harm do this again? How do we live together in the same community? How do we move ahead with life? All restorative conferencing models provide for such questions to be addressed through the facilitated encounter.

> **Victim participation must be fully voluntary.**

In each of these models, participation by the one who has been harmed must be entirely voluntary. In each, a prerequisite is that the person who caused the harm acknowledges, at least to some extent, his or her responsibility. Normally, conferences are not held if the offending person denies all responsibility, though often they do not acknowledge full responsibility prior to the conference.

Efforts are made to maximize the offending person's voluntary participation as well. Certainly conferences should not be held if he or she is unwilling and uncooperative. In reality, however, there is often some pressure on the offending person to choose between lesser evils. In interviews, those who have offended often suggest that it is difficult and frightening to face the ones they have harmed. Indeed, most of us would try to avoid such obligations if we could.

With the exception of the New Zealand family group conferences, the models described below are usually used on a discretionary, referral basis. For lesser offenses, referrals sometimes come from the community, perhaps from a school or religious institution. Occasionally, referrals are generated by the parties themselves.

Most referrals, however, come from within the justice system with the exact referral point varying with the case and the community. Cases may be referred by the police, by the prosecutor, by probation, by the court, even by prisons. In the case of a court referral, it may be after adjudication but before sentencing. In such instances, the judge takes the outcome of the conference into account in the sentence. In some cases or jurisdictions, the judge orders restitution and asks that the amount be established through a restorative conference. The agreement then becomes part of the sentence and/or the probation order.

A number of communities are now encouraging some form of restorative encounter to happen much earlier in the process, before charges have been formally brought, as a way of keeping cases out of the system. In Concord, Massachusetts, Communities for Restorative Justice represents a partnership between the police and the community and is making this possible for a variety of cases.

Originally established to help address racial disparities in the juvenile justice system in Oakland, California, pre-charge conferences based on New Zealand's model are diverting rather serious offenses out of the system by providing accountability as well as support from families and the community. With the agreement of the prosecutor, this program is able to make a "reverse Miranda" statement to the offending person, i.e., that nothing said in the conference will be used against him or her.

In one high-profile murder case in Florida, a pre-charge conference allowed the family members of the young woman who was killed, the young man who was responsible along with his family, the prosecutor, and the defense attorney to meet together to address the issues noted above and to work toward a consensus on the sentence that would be part of a plea agreement.[2]

In the U.S., however, most current programs for victim-offender encounters in cases of severe violence are outside the formal justice system and are designed to be initiated by the parties themselves, most commonly by those who have been victimized or their loved ones. At least half of U.S. states now have protocols and/or programs in place for victims who wish to participate.

Models differ in the "who" and the "how"

Although similar in basic outline, the models of restorative justice practice differ in the number and category of participants and, in some cases, the style of facilitation.

Victim offender conferences

Victim offender conferences (VOC) involve primarily those directly harmed and those responsible for the harm. Upon referral, the two parties are first worked with individually. Then, upon their agreement to proceed, they are brought together in a meeting or conference. The meeting is put together and led by a trained facilitator or co-facilitators who guide the process in a balanced manner.

A signed restitution agreement is often an outcome, although this is less likely to be true in cases of severe violence. Family members of either party may participate, but they are usually seen as having secondary, supporting roles. Persons representing the community may be involved as facilitators and/or program overseers, but they do not usually participate in meetings.

Family group conferences

Family group conferences (FGC) enlarge the circle of primary participants to include family members or other individuals significant to the parties directly involved. Because this model has tended to focus on supporting those who have offended in taking responsibility and changing their behavior, the offending person's family and/or other relevant people from the community are especially important. However, family and supporters of those harmed are invited as well. In some circumstances, and especially when the FGC is empowered to affect the legal outcome of the case, a justice person such as a police officer may be present.

Two basic forms of family group conferences have gained prominence. One model that has received considerable attention in North America was initially developed by police in Australia, based in part on ideas from New Zealand. Often this approach has used a standardized, "scripted" model of facilitation. Facilitators may be authority figures such as specially trained police officers, although though this has been controversial, especially in communities where relationships with police are strained.

This tradition or approach has given special attention to the dynamics of shame and often actively attempts to use shame in a positive way. The proactive use of shame is a highly controversial subject, however. Some argue that shame is too volatile and dangerous to encourage addressing it in a conference, even though it is very likely to be present, often for both parties.

Successful conferences involve managing rather than promoting shame.

The success of conferences seems to hinge on the successful management and transformation of shame rather than the deliberate encouragement of shame.

The older model of FGCs, and the one with which I am more familiar, originated in New Zealand and today provides the norm for juvenile justice in that country. Because this model is less well-known than other forms, at least in the United States, I will describe it somewhat more thoroughly than the others.

Responding to a crisis in the welfare and justice system for juveniles, and criticized by the indigenous Maori population for utilizing an imposed, alien, colonial system, New Zealand revolutionized its juvenile justice system in 1989. While the court system remains as a backup, the intended "default" response to most serious juvenile crime in New Zealand today is an FGC.[3]

Consequently, family group conferences can be seen as both a system of justice and as a mode of encounter in New Zealand.

Conferences are put together and facilitated by paid social service personnel called youth justice coordinators. It is their job to help families determine who should be present and to design the process that will be appropriate for them. One of the goals of the process is to be culturally appropriate, and the form of the conference is supposed to be adapted to the needs and cultures of all involved.

This is not a scripted model of facilitation. While there is often a common overall progression in the conferences, each is adapted to the needs of its particular parties. An element common to most conferences is a family caucus sometime during the conference. Here the one who has offended and her or his family go to another room to discuss what has happened and to develop a proposal to bring back to those who have been harmed and the rest of the conference.

Like the facilitator in a VOC, the coordinator of a FGC must seek to be impartial, or perhaps more accurately, equally partial to both sides, balancing the concerns and interests of all. However, he or she is charged with making sure a plan is developed that addresses causes as well as reparation, that holds the offender adequately accountable, and that is realistic.

While the community is not explicitly included, these conferences are more inclusive than VOCs. Family members of the offending person are an essential part and play very important roles—indeed, this is seen as a family empowerment model. Those who have been victimized may bring family members or victim advocates. A special attorney or youth advocate may be present, and other caregivers may be as well. In addition, since the police play a prosecutorial role in New Zealand, they must be represented.

Family group conferences, New Zealand style, are not designed simply to allow for the expression of facts and feelings and to develop restitution agreements. Because they normally take the place of a court, they are charged with developing the entire plan for the young person who offended that, in addition to reparations, includes elements of prevention and sometimes punishment. Even the actual charges may be negotiated in this meeting. Interestingly, the plan is intended to be the consensus of everyone in the confer-

> **New Zealand FGCs address both reparation and prevention.**

ence. The victim, the offender, or the police can each block an outcome if one of them is unsatisfied.

Family group conferences, then, enlarge the circle of participants to include family members or other significant people and perhaps justice officials as well. At least in the New Zealand form, a conference involves a family caucus, and the facilitator may have an enlarged role compared to a VOC, making sure that the person who caused the harm is being held appropriately accountable. FGCs, sometimes called community or accountability conferences, are being adapted in a number of countries. They also provide the framework for some of the pre-charge diversion programs within the U.S., though the actual conference may be conducted as a circle process, described below.

Circles

Circle approaches entered the restorative justice field initially from Aboriginal communities in Canada. Judge Barry Stuart, in whose court a circle was first acknowledged in a legal ruling, has chosen the term "peacemaking circles" to describe this form. Today, circles are being used for many purposes. In addition to sentencing circles, intended to determine sentences in criminal cases, there are healing circles, circles to deal with workplace conflicts, even circles designed as forms of community dialogue.

In a circle process, participants arrange themselves in a circle. They pass a "talking piece" around the circle to assure that each person speaks, one at a time, in the order in which each is seated in the circle. One or two "circle keepers" serve as facilitators of the circle. In indigenous communities, elders play an important role in leading the circle or in offering advice and insight.

A set of values, or even a philosophy, is often articulated as part of the process—values that emphasize respect, the value of each participant, integrity, the importance of speaking from the heart, and so on.

Circles consciously enlarge the circle of participants. Those who have been harmed, those who have caused harm, their family members, and sometimes justice officials are included, but community members are essential participants as well. Sometimes these community members are invited because of their connection to or interest in the specific offense or the parties involved; sometimes they are part of an ongoing circle of volunteers from the community.

Because the community is involved, discussions within the circle are often more wide-ranging than in other restorative justice models. Participants may address situations in the community that are giving rise to the offense, the support needs of both those who have experienced and caused harm, the obligations that the community might have, community norms, or other related community issues.

Although circles initially emerged from small, homogeneous communities, they are today being used in a variety of communities, including large urban areas, and for a variety of situations besides criminal cases. Circles seem to be the predominant model in educational settings. Indeed, circle processes appear to be the closest thing to a "universal" model of addressing harm and conflict that I have seen. My graduate students, who come from many countries and traditions, often note that circles are or were used in their traditions.

Circles have wide application.

This is not the place to discuss the many forms or the relative merits of each restorative justice model. What should be noted here is that all of the above are forms of encounter. They can be differentiated, however, by the numbers and categories of stakeholders who are included and by their somewhat different styles of facilitation. Again, these forms are increasingly being blended so that the differences among them seem less significant than before.

Please note that not all restorative approaches involve a direct encounter, and not all needs can be met through an encounter. While those who have been victimized have some needs that involve the person who harmed them, they also have needs that do not. Similarly, those who offend have needs and obligations that are not directly connected to those they have harmed. Thus the following typology includes both encounter and non-encounter programs.

> **Restorative justice may not involve an encounter.**

Models differ in their goals

Another way to understand the differences between these various approaches in a criminal justice context is to examine their goals. These can be placed in three categories, though they often overlap.

Alternative or diversionary programs

These programs usually aim to divert cases from, or provide an alternative to, all or some part of the criminal justice process or sentencing. Police or prosecutors may make a referral, deferring prosecution and ultimately dropping it if the case is satisfactorily settled. A judge may refer a case to a restorative conference to sort out elements of the sentence, such as restitution. In some circle processes, the prosecutor and judge may join the community in a circle designed to develop a sentence tailored to the needs of the victim, offender, and community. In Batavia, New York, a long-standing restorative justice program has worked first with victims of severe crime, then with offenders, to develop alternative pleas, sentences, and even sometimes bail agreements. In New Zealand, of course, conferences are the norm, and courts are the alternative. Pre-charge diversion programs such as those in Oakland, California, and Concord, Massachusetts, seek to keep young people out of the system by holding the offending person accountable, addressing the environment that has contributed to the offending behavior, and meeting the needs of those who were harmed.

Healing or therapeutic programs

Increasingly, restorative programs, such as victim offender dialogue conferences, are being developed for the most severe kinds of crimes—violent assault, even rape and murder. Often the offending party in these situations is in prison. In such encounter programs, involvement is not usually designed to impact the outcome of the case. With appropriate preparation and structure, such encounters have been found to be powerful, positive experiences for both victims and offenders, regardless of who initiates them.

Not all programs in this category involve direct encounters between victims and offenders from the same incident. For example, when the person who has caused the harm is not available, or the person harmed is not ready to meet with him or her, it can be helpful for the person harmed to meet with a surrogate offender who has caused a similar harm. Or an offender may meet with a surrogate victim.

Some such programs function as a form of victim-oriented offender rehabilitation. As part of the treatment process, those who have offended are encouraged to understand and take responsibility for what they have done. Victim-impact panels, where groups of victims are given an opportunity to tell their stories to offenders, may be part of this process.

Other programs such as Bridges to Life offer multiple-session, in-prison seminars that bring victims and offenders not involved in the same case, and sometimes community members, together to explore a variety of topics and issues, for the benefit of all involved.

Transitional programs

A growing area of restorative programming has to do with transitions after prison. In both halfway houses and in prisons, programs are being designed around victim harm and offender accountability in order to help both victims and offenders as the offender returns to the community.

One model is the Circles of Support and Accountability (CSA or CoSA) developed in Canada to work with men who had committed sex offenses and were being released from prison. In much of the U.S. and Canada, those who have committed such offenses and have served their sentences are released into communities with little support for the former prisoner and with great fear from the community and those they have victimized. These individuals are often ostracized by the communities that know them best, so they move on to other communities where they are not known. Given this, their rates of recidivism can be high.

Circles of Support and Accountability gather a circle of people—former prisoners, community members, even victims of similar offenses—not only to support the person who has offended, but also to hold them accountable. Initially the interaction is intense with daily check-ins and strict guidelines for what the person can do and where the person can go. Working with the ex-prisoners to take responsibility for their behavior, while putting necessary support in place, these circles have been successful in reintegrating former prisoners while allaying community fears. This model has now expanded beyond sex offenses and is increasingly being used for prisoner re-entry generally and has been found to reduce repeat offending.

Increasingly people in prison are taking the initiative to establish restorative justice groups and/or trainings within prison, and these do not easily fit into the three categories above. Prisoners at Graterford prison in Pennsylvania, for example, have developed their own training curriculum that is used to help their peers understand and address their behavior and its consequences. In the near future they hope to take this training approach national, making it available to others. *The Little Book of Restorative Justice for People in Prison* reflects the general philosophy and approach behind this.[4]

So although the "core" restorative justice programs involve direct encounters between those harmed and those causing harm, a variety of approaches are less direct. In order to make sense of all these forms, a continuum may be helpful.

A restorative continuum

In theory, most circle or conferencing models providing a direct encounter between those harmed and those causing harm would be considered fully restorative.

Conducted properly, consistent with the principles and values of restorative justice, they meet all of the criteria laid out in the guidelines for restorative justice that I outlined earlier. But what about other approaches that claim to be restorative? What about those that don't involve a direct encounter? Are there other options within the restorative framework?

It is important to view restorative justice models along a continuum, from fully restorative to not restorative, with several points or categories in between.

Seven key questions help to analyze both the effectiveness and the extent of restorative justice models for particular situations.

Degrees of restorative justice practices: a continuum

fully restorative	mostly restorative	partially restorative	potentially restorative	pseudo- or non-restorative

1. Does the model address harms, needs, and causes for all involved?

2. Is it adequately oriented to the needs of those who have been harmed?

3. Are those who offended encouraged to take responsibility?

4. Are all relevant stakeholders involved?

5. Is there an opportunity for dialogue and participatory decision-making?

6. Is the model respectful to all parties?

7. Does the model treat all equally, maintaining awareness of and addressing imbalances of power?

While conferencing or encounter programs may be fully restorative, there are situations in which these models do not fully—or even partially—apply. What about victims in cases where offenders are not apprehended or offenders are unwilling to take responsibility?

In a restorative system, services would start immediately after a crime to address victim needs and to involve the victim, regardless of whether an offender is apprehended. Thus victim assistance, while it cannot be seen as fully restorative, is an important component of a restorative system and should be seen at least as partially restorative.

> **Restorative options are important for victims, regardless of whether an offender is identified.**

Victim impact panels, without matching victims and offenders from a specific case, allow those who experienced harm to tell their stories and encourage those who have caused harm to understand what they have done. These are an important part of a restorative approach and can be seen as partly or mostly restorative.

Similarly, what happens when someone who has offended is willing to take steps to understand and to take responsibility, but the person or persons they harmed are unavailable or unwilling? A few programs for such circumstances have been developed (such as offering opportunities to learn from those harmed and to do symbolic acts of restitution), but more should be available. While perhaps not fully restorative, these programs play an essential role in the overall system of justice.

Do offender treatment or rehabilitation programs qualify as restorative justice practices? Treatment for those who have offended can be seen as a part of prevention and, along with prisoner reintegration, has some kinship with restorative justice. However, as conventionally practiced, many efforts at treatment or rehabilitation offer little that is explicitly restorative. They could, however, function restoratively, and some do by organizing treatment around helping those who have caused harm to understand and take responsibility for it and, at the same time, giving as much attention as possible to the needs of those who have been harmed.

Depending on how it is done, offender treatment may fall into the "potentially" or "partially" categories.

> **Community service may or may not be restorative.**

Similarly, offender advocacy, prisoner re-entry programs, or religious teaching in prison are in themselves not restorative; however, they may play an important role in a restorative system, especially if they are reshaped to include a restorative framework.

In my view, community service falls into the "potentially restorative" category. As currently practiced, community service is at best an alternative form of punishment, not restorative justice. In New Zealand, however, community service often is part of the outcome of a family group conference. All in the group have participated in developing the plan, the work is connected to the offense as much as possible, and within the plan are specifics about how the community and family will support and monitor the agreement. Here it has potential for being seen as repayment or a contribution to the community, mutually agreed upon by all participants. With this kind of re-framing, community service may have an important place in a restorative approach.

Then there is the "pseudo-" or "non-restorative" category. "Restorative" has become such a popular term that many acts and efforts are being labeled "restorative," but in fact they are not. Some of these might be rescued. Others cannot. The death penalty, which causes additional and irreparable harm, is one of the latter.

CHAPTER 4

Where From Here?

In my earlier writings, I often drew a sharp contrast between the retributive framework of the legal or criminal justice system and a more restorative approach to justice. Later, however, I came to realize that this polarization can be somewhat misleading. Although charts that highlight contrasting characteristics illuminate important elements differentiating the two approaches, they also hide important similarities and areas of collaboration.

Retributive justice vs. restorative justice

Philosopher of law Conrad Brunk has argued that on the theoretical or philosophical level, retribution and restoration are not the polar opposites that we often assume.[1] In fact, they have much in common. A primary goal of both retributive theory and restorative theory is to vindicate through reciprocity, by "balancing the scales." Where they differ is in what each suggests will effectively right the balance.

Both retributive and restorative theories of justice acknowledge a basic moral intuition that a balance has been thrown off by a wrongdoing. Consequently, the victim deserves something and the offender owes something. Both argue that the person who offends must be treated as a moral agent. Both approaches argue that there must be a proportional relationship between the act and the response.

> **Retribution and restoration share a concern for balance.**

They differ, however, on the currency that will fulfill the obligations and right the balance.

Retributive theory believes that pain will vindicate, but in practice that is often counterproductive for both the one harmed and the one causing harm. Restorative justice theory, on the other hand, argues that what truly vindicates is acknowledgment of a victim's harms and needs, combined with an active effort to encourage the offender to take responsibility, make right the wrongs, and address the causes of his or her behavior. By addressing this need for vindication in a positive way, restorative justice has the potential to affirm all parties and to help them transform their lives.

Criminal justice vs. restorative justice

Restorative justice advocates dream of a day when justice is fully restorative. Whether this is realistic is debatable, at least in the immediate future. More attainable, perhaps, is a time when restorative justice processes are the norm, while some form of the legal or criminal justice system provides the backup or alternative. Ideally, though, that backup system would be guided by restorative principles and values as well.

Society must have a system to sort out the "truth" as best it can when people deny responsibility. Some cases are simply too difficult or horrendous to be worked out by those with a direct stake in the offense. Some people involved in certain cases may choose to not be a part of working out the outcome. We must have a process that gives attention to those societal needs and obligations that go beyond the ones held by the immediate stakeholders. We also must not lose those qualities that the legal system, when operating properly, represents: the rule of law, due process, a deep regard for human rights, the orderly development of law.

Justice might be viewed as a continuum. On the one end is the Western legal or criminal justice system model. Its strengths—such as the encouragement of human rights—are substantial. Yet it has some glaring weaknesses.

A goal: be as restorative as possible.

At the other end is the restorative alternative. It, too, has important strengths. It, too, has limits, at least as it is currently conceived and practiced.

A realistic goal, perhaps, is to move as far as we can toward an approach that is restorative. In some cases or situations, we may not be able to move very far. In others, we may achieve processes and outcomes that are truly restorative. In between will be many cases and situations where both systems must be utilized, and justice is only partly restorative.[2] Meanwhile, we can dream of a day when this particular continuum is no longer relevant because all will rest on a restorative foundation.

One vision

In my own dreams, a truly restorative justice approach would involve true cooperation between communities and the justice system. We would use collaborative community-based restorative processes to keep people out of the formal system whenever possible. Within the system, lawyers (including prosecutors) would envision themselves less as gladiators out to win than as healers and problem-solvers; as Doug Noll has suggested, their job would be not only to lay out the legal options but to provide clients with a "conflict map" of the situation and the non-legal options.[3] Susan Herman has suggested that a "parallel justice" system should be available for those who are victimized, regardless of whether the offending party has been identified, helping those harmed to define and meet their needs. A parallel system could offer restorative interactions with those who have offended where desired and possible.[4] A truly independent victim assistance office would be trusted by both prosecution and defense and thus able to obtain the information victims need from both sides. Everyone in the system— from law enforcement to judges and beyond—would be asking the restorative justice questions such as these: Who has been harmed? What are their needs? Whose obligations are they? The adversarial court system and prison would be used as last resorts and would be operated on restorative principles and values as much as possible.[5] Due process protections would be built in, but in a non-adversarial manner. Everyone involved would seek to base their actions on a clear set of restorative principles and values, and outcomes would be assessed by these standards.

But that is just one dream, undoubtedly limited and flawed by my own "lens." To envision what a truly restorative "system" or approach might look like will require dialogue among many and diverse voices. As Dutch law professor Herman Bianchi used to say to the newly-developing restorative justice movement, true justice requires endless "palaver."

True justice requires ongoing dialogue.

Dreams and visions are important. As I said in the Afterward to *Changing Lenses*,[6]

> I believe in ideals. Much of the time we fall short of them, but they remain a beacon, something toward which to aim, something against which to test our actions. They point a direction. Only with a sense of direction can we know when we are off the path.

And my last paragraph of the Afterward, and of the book, was this:

> My hope is that you will understand this as a vision—a vision that is less an elusive mirage than it is an indistinct destination on a necessarily long and circuitous road.

A way of life

During the years I have been involved in this work, many people have commented that restorative justice is in fact a way of life. At first I was mystified; how can an approach designed initially to respond to crime become a life philosophy? I have concluded that it has to do with the ethical system that restorative justice embodies.

The Western criminal justice system is intended to promote important positive values—a recognition of the rights of others, the importance of certain boundaries on behavior, the centrality of human rights. But it does so in a way that is largely negative; it says that if you harm others, we will harm you. As James Gilligan has argued, it is a mirror image of the offending act.[7] Consequently, to make it humane, we have to bring in other values to govern and mitigate it. It does not, in itself, offer us a vision of the good.

Restorative justice, on the other hand, provides an inherently positive value system, a vision of how we can live together in a life-giving way. It is based on the assumption—a reminder for those of us living in an individualistic world—that we are interconnected. It reminds us that we live in relationship, that our actions impact others, that when those actions are harmful we have responsibilities.

As I noted earlier, restorative justice must be grounded in values. Many values can and have been articulated, but I like to focus on three "R" values: respect, responsibility, and relationship. The last one is foundational. It reminds us of a basic reality, one that is understood clearly in most religious and cultural traditions. It is also a foundational aspect of human nature; as Daniel

Goleman has pointed out, neuroscience is finding that we as human beings are "wired to connect" with others.[8]

Restorative justice is a river

Years ago, while living in Pennsylvania, my wife and I set out to find the source of the Susquehanna River that flows through that state. We followed one of its two branches until we arrived behind a farmer's barn and found a rusty pipe sticking out of a hill. Fed by a spring, the water fell from the pipe into a bathtub that served as a watering trough for cattle. It spilled over the bathtub, spread out along the ground, then formed the stream that eventually became a mighty river.

It is, of course, debatable whether this particular spring is *the* source. There are other springs in the vicinity that could compete for that honor. And, of course, this stream would not be a river if it were not fed by hundreds of other streams. Nevertheless, this river and this spring have become my metaphor for the restorative justice movement.

The contemporary field of restorative justice started as a tiny trickle in the 1970s, an effort by a handful of people dreaming of doing justice differently. It originated in practice and in experimentation rather than in abstractions. The theory, the concept, came later. But while the immediate sources of the modern restorative justice stream are recent, both concept and practice draw upon traditions as deep as human history and as wide as the world community.

For some time, the restorative justice stream was driven underground by our modern legal systems. In recent decades, however, that stream has resurfaced, growing into a widening river. Restorative justice today is acknowledged worldwide by governments and communities concerned about crime. Thousands of people around the globe bring their experience and expertise to the river. This river, like all rivers, exists because it is fed by numerous tributaries flowing in from around the world.

Some of the feeder streams are practical programs, such as those being implemented in many countries. The river is also being fed by a variety of indigenous traditions and current adaptations which draw upon those traditions: family group conferences inspired by Maori traditions in New Zealand, for example; sentencing circles from First Nation communities in the Canadian North; Navajo peacemaking courts; African customary law; or the Afghani practice of *jirga*. The field of mediation and conflict resolution feeds into that river, as do the victim rights and assistance movements and alternatives-to-prison movements of the past decades. A variety of religious traditions flow into this river.

While the experiments, practices, and customs from many communities and cultures are instructive, none can or should be copied and simply plugged into other communities or societies. Rather, they should be viewed as examples of how different communities and societies found their own appropriate

> **Justice processes must be context-appropriate.**

ways to express justice as a response to wrongdoing. These approaches may give us inspiration and a place to begin. While these examples and traditions may not provide blueprints, they may serve as catalysts for forming ideas and directions.

This context-oriented approach to justice reminds us that true justice emerges from conversation and takes into account local needs and traditions. This is one of the reasons why we must be very cautious about top-down strategies for implementing restorative justice.

The argument presented here is quite simple. Justice will not be served if we maintain our exclusive focus on the questions that drive our current justice systems: What laws have been broken? Who did it? What do they deserve?

True justice requires, instead, that we ask questions such as these: Who has been hurt? What do they need? Whose obligations and responsibilities are these? Who has a stake in this situation? What are the causes that have contributed to this? What is the process that can involve the stakeholders in finding a solution? Restorative justice requires us to change not just our lenses but also our questions.

Above all, restorative justice is an invitation to join in conversation so that we may support and learn from each other. It is a reminder that all of us are indeed embedded in a web of relationships.

Fundamental Principles of Restorative Justice

Howard Zehr and Harry Mika[1]

These principles, first published in 1998, are in some ways dated. For the sake of continuity, however we have decided to reproduce them in their original form. We encourage you to update and adapt them to your situation.

1.0 Crime is fundamentally a violation of people and interpersonal relationships.

   1.1 Victims and the community have been harmed and are in need of restoration.

      1.1.1 The primary victims are those most directly affected by the offense, but others, such as family members of victims and offenders, witnesses, and members of the affected community, are also victims.

      1.1.2 The relationships affected (and reflected) by crime must be addressed.

      1.1.3 Restoration is a continuum of responses to the range of needs and harms experienced by victims, offenders, and the community.

   1.2 Victims, offenders, and the affected communities are the key stakeholders in justice.

      1.2.1 A restorative justice process maximizes the input and participation of these parties—but especially primary victims as well as offenders—in the search for restoration, healing, responsibility, and prevention.

      1.2.2 The roles of these parties will vary according to the nature of the offense, as well as the capacities and preferences of the parties.

      1.2.3 The state has circumscribed roles, such as investigating facts, facilitating processes, and ensuring safety, but the state is not a primary victim.

2.0 Violations create obligations and liabilities.

2.1 Offenders' obligations are to make things right as much as possible.

2.1.1 Since the primary obligation is to victims, a restorative justice process empowers victims to effectively participate in defining obligations.

2.1.2 Offenders are provided opportunities and encouragement to understand the harm they have caused to victims and the community and to develop plans for taking appropriate responsibility.

2.1.3 Voluntary participation by offenders is maximized; coercion and exclusion are minimized. However, offenders may be required to accept their obligations if they do not do so voluntarily.

2.1.4 Obligations that follow from the harm inflicted by crime should be related to making things right.

2.1.5 Obligations may be experienced as difficult, even painful, but are not intended as pain, vengeance, or revenge.

2.1.6 Obligations to victims, such as restitution, take priority over other sanctions and obligations to the state, such as fines.

2.1.7 Offenders have an obligation to be active participants in addressing their own needs.

2.2 *The community's obligations are to victims and to offenders and for the general welfare of its members.*

2.2.1 The community has a responsibility to support and help victims of crime to meet their needs.

2.2.2 The community bears a responsibility for the welfare of its members and the social conditions and relationships that promote both crime and community peace.

2.2.3 The community has responsibilities to support efforts to integrate offenders into the community, to be actively involved in the definitions of offender obligations, and to ensure opportunities for offenders to make amends.

3.0 Restorative justice seeks to heal and put right the wrongs.

3.1 *The needs of victims for information, validation, vindication, restitution, testimony, safety, and support are the starting points of justice.*

3.1.1 The safety of victims is an immediate priority.

3.1.2 The justice process provides a framework that promotes the work of recovery and healing that is ultimately the domain of the individual victim.

3.1.3 Victims are empowered by maximizing their input and by participation in determining needs and outcomes.

3.1.4 Offenders are involved in repair of the harm insofar as possible.

3.2 The process of justice maximizes opportunities for exchange of information, participation, dialogue, and mutual consent between victim and offender.

3.2.1 Face-to-face encounters are appropriate in some instances, while alternative forms of exchange are more appropriate in others.

3.2.2 Victims have the principal role in defining and directing the terms and conditions of the exchange.

3.2.3 Mutual agreement takes precedence over imposed outcomes.

3.2.4 Opportunities are provided for remorse, forgiveness, and reconciliation.

3.3 Offenders' needs and competencies are addressed.

3.3.1 Recognizing that offenders themselves have often been harmed, healing and integration of offenders into the community are emphasized.

3.3.2 Offenders are supported and treated respectfully in the justice process.

3.3.3 Removal from the community and severe restriction of offenders is limited to the minimum necessary.

3.3.4 Justice values personal change above compliant behavior.

3.4 *The justice process belongs to the community.*

3.4.1 Community members are actively involved in doing justice.

3.4.2 The justice process draws from community resources and, in turn, contributes to the building and strengthening of community.

3.4.3 The justice process attempts to promote changes in the community to both prevent similar harms from happening to others, and to foster early intervention to address the needs of victims and the accountability of offenders.

3.5 *Justice is mindful of the outcomes, intended and unintended, of its responses to crime and victimization.*

3.5.1 Justice monitors and encourages follow-through since healing, recovery, accountability, and change are maximized when agreements are kept.

3.5.2 Fairness is assured, not by uniformity of outcomes, but through provision of necessary support and opportunities to all parties as well as avoidance of discrimination based on ethnicity, class, and sex.

3.5.3 Outcomes that are predominately deterrent or incapacitative should be implemented as a last resort, involving the least restrictive intervention while seeking restoration of the parties involved.

3.5.4 Unintended consequences, such as the cooptation of restorative processes for coercive or punitive ends, undue offender orientation, or the expansion of social control, are resisted.

APPENDIX II

Restorative Justice in Threes

Howard Zehr

3 assumptions underlie restorative justice:
- When people and relationships are harmed, needs are created;
- The needs created by harms lead to obligations;
- The obligation is to heal and "put right" the harms; this is a just response.

3 principles of restorative justice reflect these assumptions. A just response:

- Repairs the harm caused by, and revealed by, wrongdoing (restoration);
- Encourages appropriate responsibility for addressing needs and repairing the harm (accountability);
- Involves those impacted, including the community, in the resolution (engagement).

3 underlying *values* provide the foundation:
- Respect;
- Responsibility;
- Relationship.

3 questions are central to restorative justice:
- Who has been hurt?
- What are their needs?
- Who has the obligation to address the needs, to put right the harms, to restore relationships?

(As opposed to: What rules were broken? Who did it? What do they deserve?)

3 stakeholder groups should be considered and/or involved:
- Those who have been harmed, and their families;
- Those who have caused harm, and their families;
- The relevant community or communities.

3 aspirations guide restorative justice: the desire to live in right relationship:
- With one another;
- With the creation;
- With the creator.

APPENDIX III

Restorative Justice? What's That?

Howard Zehr

Do a Google search for the phrase "restorative justice," and you will get over a million hits—and this for a term that was virtually non-existent 35 years ago. Ask what it means, and you may get a variety of answers.

For many, it implies a meeting between victims of crime and those who have committed those crimes. A family meets with the teenagers who burglarized their home, expressing their feelings and negotiating a plan for repayment. Parents meet with the man who murdered their daughter to tell him the impact and get answers to their questions. A school principal and his family meet with the boys who exploded a pipe bomb in their front yard, narrowly missing the principal and his infant child. The family's and the neighbors' fears of a recurrence are put to rest, and the boys for the first time understand the enormity of what they have done.

Restorative justice does include encounter programs for those harmed and those causing harm; today there are thousands of such programs all over the world. But restorative justice is more than an encounter, and its scope reaches far beyond the criminal justice system. Increasingly schools are implementing restorative disciplinary processes, religious bodies are using restorative approaches to deal with wrongdoing—including clergy sexual abuse—and whole societies are considering restorative approaches to address wrongs done on a mass scale. Of growing popularity are restorative conferences or circle processes that bring groups of people together to share perspectives and concerns and collaboratively find solutions to the problems facing their families and communities.

Restorative justice emerged in the 1970s as an effort to correct some of the weaknesses of the Western legal system while building on its strengths. An area of special concern has been the neglect of victims and their needs; legal justice is largely about what to do with offenders. It has also been driven by a desire to hold those who cause harm truly accountable. Recognizing that punishment is often ineffective, restorative justice aims at helping those who offend to recognize the harm they have caused and encouraging them to repair the harm, to the extent it is possible. Rather than obsessing about whether those who offend get what they deserve, restorative justice focuses on repairing the harm of crime and engaging individuals and community members in the process.

It is basically common sense—the kind of lessons our parents and fore-parents taught—and that has led some to call it a way of life. When a wrong has been done, it needs to be named and acknowledged. Those who have been harmed need to be able to grieve their losses, to be able to tell their stories, to have their questions answered—that is, to have the harms and needs caused by the offense addressed. They—and we—need to have those who have done wrong accept their responsibility and take steps to repair the harm to the extent it is possible.

As you might imagine with so many Google references, the usage of the term varies widely. Sometimes it is used in ways that are rather far removed from what those in the field have intended. So when you see the term, you might ask yourself these questions: Are the wrongs being acknowledged? Are the needs of those who were harmed being addressed? Is the one who committed the harm being encouraged to understand the damage and accept his or her obligation to make right the wrong? Are those involved in or affected by this being invited to be part of the "solution"? Is concern being shown for everyone involved? If the answers to these questions are "no," then even though it may have restorative elements, it isn't restorative justice.

APPENDIX IV

Ten Ways to Live Restoratively

Howard Zehr[1]

1. Take relationships seriously, envisioning yourself in an interconnected web of people, institutions, and the environment.

2. Try to be aware of the impact—potential as well as actual—of your actions on others and the environment.

3. When your actions negatively impact others, take responsibility by acknowledging and seeking to

repair the harm—even when you could probably get away with avoiding or denying it.

4. Treat everyone respectfully, even those you don't expect to encounter again, even those you feel don't deserve it, even those who have harmed or offended you or others.

5. Involve those affected by a decision, as much as possible, in the decision-making process.

6. View the conflicts and harms in your life as opportunities.

7. Listen, deeply and compassionately, to others, seeking to understand even if you don't agree with them. (Think about who you want to be in the latter situation rather than just being right.)

8. Engage in dialogue with others, even when what is being said is difficult, remaining open to learning from them and the encounter.

9. Be cautious about imposing your "truths" and views on other people and situations.

10. Sensitively confront everyday injustices including sexism, racism, homophobia, and classism.

The chart below explores some implications of five key restorative justice principles for criminal justice and for restorative living.

Restorative Justice Principles adapted by Catherine Bargen from Susan Sharpe, *Restorative Justice: A Vision for Healing and Change*. Thanks to Catherine for her suggestions on the above as well.

Principle of Restorative Justice	Application for Criminal Justice	Application for Restorative Living
Invite full participation and consensus.	Victims, offenders, and the community have a voice in responding to criminal harm, with as much agreement as possible in what the outcome should look like.	All those who feel they have a stake in a situation of harm or conflict can be invited to participate in dialogue around the issues and have a voice in the outcomes or decisions made. Power imbalances are noted and addressed as much as possible to achieve consensus.
Heal what has been broken.	When a crime is committed, the need for healing inevitably arises. This may take the form of emotional healing (for victims and for offenders), relationship healing, and/or reparation of property damage.	Our everyday interactions and situations can result in hurtful words and actions, which may create feelings of injustice or imbalance in our relationships. As much as possible, the restorative approach seeks to bring those hurts to light and create space for healing and reparation.
Seek full and direct accountability.	Offenders need to take responsibility for their own actions and choices. They are given the opportunity to explain their behavior and fulfill the obligations created from their behavior directly to the people they have harmed.	When harm occurs, we can nurture an environment where we are encouraged to take ownership for our own roles in hurtful behavior or abuses of power. Living restoratively means respectfully expecting oneself and others to be accountable for our actions in ways that are fair and reasonable.

Principle of Restorative Justice	Application for Criminal Justice	Application for Restorative Living
Reunite what has been divided.	Victims of crime often experience a sense of isolation from the community, as do offenders. While the reasons for this isolation may differ between these two groups, processes that allow for reintegration need to be sought in the wake of a crime for all that have been affected. Such processes can create a renewed sense of wholeness and "closure," as well as a sense of reintegration into the community.	Hurtful or damaging behavior in our places of interaction can create feelings of isolation and of being an outcast. It can result in individuals taking sides and developing an "us/them" mentality. As much as possible, restorative living aims to take stock of where divisions have occurred in our communities and to work toward balance, understanding, and reconciliation.
Strengthen the community to prevent future harms.	A justice process that is restorative will focus not only on the details of the crime at hand, but what the systemic causes of crime are in the community and how they can be addressed. In this way, a healthier and safer community is created for all, not just those wanting to be protected from crime.	Most communities can ultimately use situations of harm to learn, grow, and change where necessary. When living restoratively, we can help illuminate systemic injustice and power imbalances. We then advocate for positive changes in order to make the community a healthier and more just place for all.

Restorative Justice and Peacebuilding

At the Center for Justice and Peacebuilding, where I am on the faculty, we envision the peacebuilding field as a broad umbrella term. As my colleague Lisa Schirch explains in *The Little Book of Strategic Peacebuilding* (Good Books, 2004), it encompasses a wide range of fields, programs, and approaches aimed at creating a just and peaceful society.

One way of defining peacebuilding is that it is about building and maintaining healthy relationships and mending those that have been broken. Given that focus, restorative justice can be viewed as adding the following specific contributions to peacebuilding and to fields within peacebuilding such as conflict resolution or transformation:

1. Recognition that conflict involves injustices that must be addressed;

2. A relational understanding of wrongdoing that focuses on the impact on people and relationships rather than rules;

3. A set of principles to guide us when a harm or wrong has occurred;

4. A group of specific practices that, although they use some skill sets similar to those for conflict resolution, allow participants to name and address the harms involved and the resulting obligations;

5. An explicit grounding in core values and principles that guide the process and are fundamental for healthy relationships.

ENDNOTES

Chapter 1

[1] Howard Zehr, *Transcending: Reflections of Crime Victims* (Good Books, 2001), 9.

[2] A fuller treatment of the justice needs of victims may be found in Zehr, *Transcending: Reflections of Crime Victims,* Part 2.

[3] Shame theory has emerged as an important topic in restorative justice. In his pioneering book, *Crime, shame and reintegration* (Cambridge University Press, 1989), John Braithwaite argues that shame that stigmatizes pushes people toward crime. Shame may be "re-integrative," however, when it denounces the offense but not the offender and opportunities are provided for the shame to be removed or transformed. The topic is highly controversial, however, and the best research suggests that shame is indeed a factor in both victimization and offending, but it has to be handled very carefully. In most situations, the focus needs to be on managing or transforming shame rather than imposing it.

[4] See Carolyn Yoder, *The Little Book of Trauma Healing* (Good Books, 2005).

[5] See Kay Pranis, *The Little Book of Circle Processes* (Good Books, 2005), and Kay Pranis, Barry Stuart, and Mark Wedge, *Peacemaking Circles: From Crime to Community* (Living Justice Press, 2003).

Chapter 2

[1] See http://emu.edu/now/restorative-justice/, May 2, 2013 as
well as Ross London, *Crime, Punishment, and Restorative Justice:
From the Margins to the Mainstream* (Lynne Rienner Publishers,
2010).

[2] An overview of this debate may be found in Gerry Johnstone,
Restorative Justice: Ideas, Values, Debates (Willan, 2002), 136ff.
This book provides a helpful overview and analysis of the
debates and critical issues in the field of restorative justice.

[3] The role of the state is most contested in situations where
minority groups have felt systematically oppressed by the
government (e.g., in Northern Ireland or much of urban
America) or where the state is viewed as having coopted
restorative justice while implementing it from the top down.
The latter has been a particular concern of community and
indigenous groups, for example, in New Zealand and Canada.

[4] James Gilligan, *Violence: Reflections on a National Epidemic*
(Random House, 1996).

[5] Sandra Bloom, *Creating Sanctuary: Toward the Evolution of Sane
Societies* (Routledge, 1997). See also Carolyn Yoder, *The Little
Book of Trauma Healing* (Good Books, 2005).

[6] Jarem Sawatsky, *Justpeace Ethics: A Guide to Restorative Justice and
Peacebuilding* (Cascade Books, 2009).

[7] This is an adaptation of Tony Marshall's widely cited definition:
"Restorative justice is a process whereby all parties with a
stake in a specific offense come together to resolve collectively
how to deal with the aftermath of the offense and its
implications for the future."

[8] Susan Sharpe, *Restorative Justice: A Vision for Healing and Change*
(Edmonton, Alberta: Mediation and Restorative Justice
Centre, 1998).

[9] The word "closure" is often offensive to victims, especially
victims of severe crime. It seems to suggest that all can be
put behind and the book closed, and that is not possible.

However, the word also implies a sense of being able to move forward, which restorative justice aims to make possible.

[10] These signposts were originally published, in a somewhat different version, as a bookmark by Mennonite Central Committee, Akron, Pennsylvania, in 1997. I have made slight modifications in this edition.

Chapter 3

[1] See http://peace.fresno.edu/docs/APeacemakingModel.pdf.

[2] See http://www.nytimes.com/2013/01/06/magazine/can-forgiveness-play-a-role-in-criminal-justice.html.

[3] The youth justice system in New Zealand is designed to divert offenders in less serious cases out of the system, avoiding both a formal FGC and court. (This is sometimes done in conjunction with an informal victim offender conference.) This design is based on the assumptions that much youth offending is part of a developmental stage and that entering youth into the formal system may encourage future offending behavior.

[4] Barb Toews, *The Little Book of Restorative Justice for People in Prison* (Good Books, 2006).

Chapter 4

[1] Conrad Brunk, "Restorative Justice and the Philosophical Theories of Criminal Punishment" in *The Spiritual Roots of Restorative Justice,* Michael L. Hadley, editor (State University of New York Press, 2001), 31-56.

[2] In *Restorative Justice and Responsive Regulation* (Oxford University Press, 2002), John Braithwaite suggests an interesting model for how restoration, deterrence, and incapacitation might be addressed in restorative justice.

[3] Doug Noll, *Peacemaking: Practicing at the Intersection of Law and Human Conflict* (Cascadia, 2003).

[4] Susan Herman, *Parallel Justice for Victims of Crime* (National Center for Victims of Crime, 2010).

[5] For example, in *The Legacy of Community Justice*, edited by Sandra Pavelka, Anne Seymour, and Barry Stuart (Vernon, British Columbia: JCharlton Publishing Ltd, 2013), Dennis Maloney, Gordon Bazemore, and Joe Hudson outline the way probation might be reshaped so that probation officers become "community justice officers" who facilitate community responses to crime and mobilize community resources. Also of interest is Judge Fred McElrea's chapter, "Restorative Justice as a Procedural Revolution: Some Lessons from the Adversary System" in *Civilising Criminal Justice: An International Restorative Agenda for Penal Reform* (Waterside Press, U.K., 2013). Among other suggestions, Judge McElrea calls for community justice centers where community members could take their cases directly instead of going through the formal justice process.

[6] Howard Zehr, *Changing Lenses: A New Focus for Crime and Justice* (Herald Press, 1990, 1995, 2005).

[7] James Gilligan, *Violence: Reflections on a National Epidemic* (Random House, 1996).

[8] Daniel Goleman, *Social Intelligence: The New Science of Human Relationships* (Bantam, 2007).

Appendix I

[1] Howard Zehr and Harry Mika, "Fundamental Principles of Restorative Justice," *The Contemporary Justice Review,* Vol. 1, No. 1 (1998), 47-55.

Appendix IV

[1] See http://emu.edu/now/restorative-justice/2009/11/27/10-ways-to-live-restoratively/.

Additional Reading

Little Books of Justice & Peacebuilding
related to restorative justice

David R. Karp, *The Little Book of Restorative Justice for Colleges and Universities.*

Allan MacRae and Howard Zehr, *The Little Book of Family Group Conferences, New Zealand Style.*

Kay Pranis, *The Little Book of Circle Processes.*

Lorraine Stutzman Amstutz, *The Little Book of Victim Offender Conferencing.*

Lorraine Stutzman Amstutz and Judy H. Mullet, *The Little Book of Restorative Discipline for Schools.*

Barb Toews, *The Little Book of Restorative Justice for People in Prison.*

Carolyn Yoder, *The Little Book of Trauma Healing.*

Howard Zehr, *El Pequeño Libro De Justicia Restaurativa.*

Related resources by the author

Changing Lenses: A New Focus for Crime and Justice
(Herald Press, 1990, 1995, 2005).

Doing Life: Reflections of Men and Women Serving Life Sentences
(Good Books, 1996, 2010).

Transcending: Reflections of Crime Victims
(Good Books, 2001).

What Will Happen to Me? with Lorraine Stutzman Amstutz
(Good Books, 2011).

Critical Issues in Restorative Justice, with Barb Toews
(Lynne Rienner, 2004).

"Restorative Justice Blog," with Carl Stauffer, available at
http://emu.edu/now/restorative-justice/.

The Zehr Institute for Restorative Justice
(webinar series and other resources) available at
http://emu.edu/cjp/restorative-justice/.

About the Author

Howard Zehr has been called the "grandfather" of restorative justice, beginning his work as a practitioner and theorist in the late 1970s at the foundational stage of the field. He directed the first formal victim offender conferencing program in the U.S. and is one of the original developers of restorative justice as a concept. A prolific writer and editor, speaker, educator, and photojournalist, Zehr actively mentors other leaders in the field.

His book *Changing Lenses: A New Focus for Crime and Justice* is considered a foundational work in restorative justice. His many other publications include *Doing Life: Reflections of Men and Women Serving Life Sentences*; *Transcending: Reflections of Crime Victims*; and *What Will Happen to Me?* He has spoken and trained others throughout North America and in more than 25 other countries.

Zehr is Distinguished Professor of Restorative Justice and co-director of the Zehr Institute for Restorative Justice at The Center for Justice and Peacebuilding, Eastern Mennonite University (Harrisonburg, Virginia). Zehr received his B.A. from Morehouse College, his M.A. from the University of Chicago, and his Ph.D. from Rutgers University.

Group Discounts for

The Little Book of Restorative Justice Revised & Updated
ORDER FORM

If you would like to order multiple copies of *The Little Book of Restorative Justice* by Howard Zehr for groups you know or are a part of, please email **bookorders@skyhorsepublishing.com** or fax order to **(212) 643-6819**. (Discounts apply only for more than one copy.)

Photocopy this page and the next as often as you like.

The following discounts apply:

1 copy	$5.99
2-5 copies	$5.39 each (a 10% discount)
6-10 copies	$5.09 each (a 15% discount)
11-20 copies	$4.79 each (a 20% discount)
21-99 copies	$4.19 each (a 30% discount)
100 or more	$3.59 each (a 40% discount)

Free Shipping for orders of 100 or more!
Prices subject to change.

Quantity   *Price*   *Total*

_____ copies of **Restorative Justice** @ _____ _____

(Standard ground shipping costs will be added for orders of less than 100 copies.)

METHOD OF PAYMENT

❏   Check or Money Order
        *(payable to **Skyhorse Publishing** in U.S. funds)*

❏   Please charge my:
    ❏ MasterCard   ❏ Visa
    ❏ Discover ❏ American Express

\# _____

Exp. date and sec. code_____

Signature _____

Name _____

Address _____

City_____

State _____

Zip_____

Phone_____

Email _____

SHIP TO: (if different)
Name _____

Address _____

City_____

State _____

Zip_____

Call: (212) 643-6816
Fax: (212) 643-6819
Email: bookorders@skyhorsepublishing.com
(do not email credit card info)